# Sixty 60 Days
# of Prayer for Iran

## Based on
## The Psalms of David

## Rev. Dr. Mohsen Kazemi

To

**The people of Iran and my Lord and Savior, Jesus Christ**

# Acknowledgement

I am deeply grateful to my dear sister in faith, Feri, who wholeheartedly translated these words. I would like to thank Hee Jung Son, Moira and Richard Brown and Mary Hogan for their wonderful editorial help.

My special gratitude to my soulmate and best fan, my wife, Insook Koh.

This book would not have been created without the guidance of my Lord Jesus and His Holy Spirit.

# Table of Contents

# Introduction

The collection you are holding is drawn from sixty days of prayers for Iran. These prayers were originally shared as daily devotionals on the YouTube channel of Mohabat Church, during a time of hardship and struggle in Iran, calling on the faithful to pray for the country.

This book is designed for daily prayer over sixty consecutive days for Iran and its people. Please use it as a guide for daily prayer, and refrain from reading it all in one day.

Scriptures are from The Holy Bible, New King James Version (1982). Thomas Nelson Publishers.

I pray that the Lord Jesus will swiftly answer our prayers for Iran and its people. My prayer for you, dear readers, is that through this book and these prayers, your relationship with the Father, Jesus Christ, and the Holy Spirit will grow stronger, and that you may become ever more steadfast in your faith.

# First Day
## The Lord is my refuge; whom shall I fear?

Our devotional today comes from Psalm 27:

As our fellow countrymen in Iran face persecution and hardship at this time, let us come before the Lord together and pray Psalm 27—for ourselves, our loved ones in Iran, our nation, and its leaders:

*¹The LORD is my light and my salvation; whom shall I fear? The LORD is the strength of my life; of whom shall I be afraid? ²When the wicked came against me. To eat up my flesh, my enemies and foes, they stumbled and fell. ³Though an army may encamp against me, my heart shall not fear; though war may rise against me, in this I will be confident. ⁴One thing I have desired of the LORD, that will I seek: that I may dwell in the house of the LORD all the days of my life, to behold the beauty of the LORD, and to inquire in His temple. ⁵For in the time of trouble, He shall hide me in His pavilion; in the secret place of His tabernacle, He shall hide me; He shall set me high upon a rock. ⁶And now my head shall be lifted up above my enemies all around me; therefore, I will offer sacrifices of joy in His tabernacle. I will sing, yes, I will sing praises to the LORD.*

Amen

In times of hardship, persecution, and every challenge, our Lord Jesus Christ is our light and salvation— the Lord who is the refuge of our souls. When evildoers, adversaries, and enemies rise against us, if we stand firm in the Lord, it is they who will stumble and fall. Scripture says, *"Though an army encamps against me, my heart will not fear; though war breaks out against me, I will remain confident."* The Lord will shelter us in times of trouble, set us high upon a rock beyond the reach of harm, and lift our heads above our enemies. Then, with joyful hearts, we will sing and offer praise in His presence.

For those whose loved ones and compatriots in Iran are enduring persecution and facing danger, let us offer this prayer on their behalf:

Father, Lord, O Father, You see all things, and nothing is hidden from You. Jesus Christ has taught us to pray for our enemies. Therefore, Lord, we pray for the leaders and rulers of Iran: open their eyes and ears to the truth and to love. In the name of the Lord Jesus Christ, Father, protect the people of Iran under Your divine protection.

O Father, just as You prophesied in Jeremiah 49 regarding Iran and Elam, saying that You would establish Your throne there and reign, You have already begun Your work.

Now, O Lord Jesus Christ, reign in love, reign in Iran, and save the people of Iran. Save, O Lord. Bring the adversaries and enemies to know You, that they too may be saved. Lord, grant patience to the oppressed, to those whose loved ones have been killed or harmed. Renew their hearts with Your presence and love. We stand together and pray, Father, have mercy on the people of Iran and bring an end to this war, conflict, and injustice. Be with each of us, that we may stand firm against fear, glorify You alone, and remember that wherever we are, You have not given us a spirit of fear, but a spirit of adoption, by which we cry, "Abba, Father!" Father, help us. We place our trust in You in all things and believe that You work all things together for good for those who love You and are called according to Your purpose.

In the name of Jesus Christ,

Amen

Dear ones keep Iran, its people, and its government in your prayers. May the Lord be with you. Amen

# Second Day
# Father, You are the fortress and refuge of the Iranian People

Our devotional today is based on Psalm 91:

In these challenging times for our country and our fellow citizens, we turn to Psalm 91 as a prayer for our people and the injustice they are enduring, asking our Heavenly Father to remove this injustice. May the people of Iran, especially those who are suffering, turn to the Lord Jesus Christ, and may He bring an end to their suffering soon.

*[1]He who dwells in the secret place of the Most High, shall abide under the shadow of the Almighty. [2]I will say of the Lord, "He is my refuge and my fortress; my God, in Him I will trust." [3]Surely He shall deliver you from the snare of the fowler, and from the perilous pestilence. [4]He shall cover you with His feathers, and under His wings you shall take refuge; His truth shall be your shield and buckler. [5]You shall not be afraid of the terror by night, nor of the arrow that flies by day, [6]nor of the pestilence that walks in darkness, nor of the destruction that lays waste at noonday. [7]A thousand may fall at your side, and ten thousand at your right hand; but it shall not come near you. [8]Only with your eyes shall you look and see the reward of the wicked. [9]Because you have made the Lord, who is my refuge, even the Most High, your dwelling place, [10]no evil shall befall you, nor shall any plague come near your dwelling; [11]For He shall give His angels charge over you, to keep you in all your ways. [12]In their hands they shall bear you up, lest you dash your foot against a stone. [13]You shall tread upon the lion and the cobra, the young lion and the serpent you shall trample underfoot. [14]"Because he has set his love upon Me, therefore I will deliver him; I will set him on high, because he*

*has known My name.* <sup>15</sup>*He shall call upon Me, and I will answer him;* <sup>16</sup>*with long life I will satisfy him and show him My salvation."*

Amen

O Father, in the name of Jesus Christ, we lift up the people of Iran before You. We bring before You the injustice, suffering, killings, and crimes they are enduring. Lord, You know all things, O Father, and all is within Your sovereign hands. We ask, Father, that You do not allow this injustice and suffering to continue. O Lord, help the people of Iran. As Your Word promises, protect them under Your wings. Send Your angels to guard and support them.

O Lord, open their eyes to see You, open their ears to hear Your beautiful voice, and turn them from their wicked ways. We also bring before You, O Lord, the leaders and rulers of Iran. In the name of Jesus Christ, transform their hearts of stone into hearts of flesh. Lead them to know You and change their ways, that they may no longer oppress the people.

Do Your work, O Father, because You know better than anyone that You alone can answer this injustice once and for all, bringing it to an end. Just as, O Lord, You brought down the communist wall overnight without bloodshed, You are able, Father—only You, O Jesus Christ—to bring down this wall of injustice and suffering without violence, and reign over our land.

Pour out Your love and grace upon the nation of Iran. We lift up those who are suffering and broken-hearted, O Lord. You alone are the healer of broken- hearts, and You alone can heal all sickness and suffering. Complete the work You have begun in Iran, O Lord, and deliver the people from this injustice and suffering.

In the name of Jesus Christ,

Amen

6

# Third Day
## The Lord is able

The Elyam Worship Group has issued a call for Christians to unite in prayer. Their message is profoundly true: our strength lies in prayer, especially in times of attack from enemies and when kings, governments, and people endure oppression. As I have often shared, and as the book of Ephesians reminds us, *"Our struggle is not against flesh and blood, but against heavenly forces and demonic forces, against the powers of this dark world."* Prayer and intercession are the most powerful weapons available to us as Christians. We are called to stand as intercessors, lifting others in prayer before the Lord.

Throughout both the Old and New Testaments, whenever God's people humble themselves, seek His presence, and pray, the Lord—who is the Lord of hosts, the Almighty—is both able and willing to bring deliverance, salvation, healing, and blessings for His people. As Christians, we are called to pray for those who are suffering, just as 1 Corinthians 6 teaches us to lift up our brothers and sisters when they are in distress, to pray for them, and to personally go to their aid. Let us now come together in prayer for our land, our homeland, the people of Iran, and its government. Let us kneel and pray:

O Lord, our Father, You are all-powerful. Your Word in Proverbs 21 tells us that the heart of kings is in the hands of the Lord, and You turn it wherever You will, like streams of water. O Lord, You are able to change hearts. You can change the hearts of the rulers of Iran and cause all things to work together for good and for Your glory. Father, as intercessors, as Your sons and daughters, we come before You to pray for Iran and the Iranian people. O Lord, bring an end to the oppression in this land. End the injustice, suffering, and bloodshed in our country. We lift up the Iranians who are enduring this oppression, and in the name of Jesus Christ, we ask that You protect them with Your angels.

O Lord, we stand in opposition to the demonic powers at work, seeking to destroy and oppress. In the name of Jesus Christ, the Lord who went to the cross for our salvation and triumphed over Satan and death through His resurrection, we rebuke these evil forces. We stand firm in the name of Jesus Christ and declare, O Lord, precious Christ, pour out Your love and protection upon Iran and its people. O Lord of Hosts, arise, arise, and fulfill Your work in Iran and in the lives of the Iranian people. Bring an end to this injustice and oppression.

In the name of Jesus Christ,

Amen

# Fourth Day
## O Lord Jehovah, arise and save Iran

In these challenging times, as our nation and its people endure oppression, let us unite in prayer for sixty days, interceding with the Word of God for our country, its people, and their freedom. Let us earnestly seek the Lord's presence, petitioning that He not withhold His help from the people of Iran and its land. May His light shine in this darkness, may He grant salvation to the people, and may He bring an end to injustice and oppression. Today's message is from Psalm 109:

*[1]Do not keep silent, O God of my praise! [2]For the mouth of the wicked and the mouth of the deceitful have opened against me; they have spoken against me with a lying tongue. [3]They have also surrounded me with words of hatred and fought against me without a cause. [4]In return for my love they are my accusers, but I give myself to prayer. [5]Thus they have rewarded me evil for good, and hatred for my love.*

And then He says:

*[21]But You, O God the Lord, deal with me for Your name's sake; because Your mercy is good, deliver me. [22]For I am poor and needy, and my heart is wounded within me. [23]I am gone like a shadow when it lengthens; I am shaken off like a locust. [24]My knees are weak through fasting, and my flesh is feeble from lack of fatness. [25]I also have become a reproach to them; when they look at me, they shake their heads. [26]Help me, O Lord my God! Oh, save me according to Your mercy, [27]that they may know that this is Your hand— that You, Lord, have done it! [28]Let them curse, but You bless; when they arise, let them be ashamed, but let Your servant rejoice. [29]Let my accusers be clothed with shame and let them cover themselves with their own disgrace as with a mantle.*

Let this be our prayer for Iran and the Iranian people, and for all our compatriots who are suffering:

O Lord, O Jehovah, O Father, for the sake of Your name, act on behalf of the people of Iran and its land. Because Your love is good, and Your love extends from earth to heaven. O Lord, the Iranians are poor and in need, not only in physical poverty but also spiritually destitute. All are in need; every heart is broken, wounded by oppression and injustice.

This suffering has endured so long that it feels as though the people are being destroyed, their shadows growing ever longer[1]. They are like locusts, shaken by hardship, their knees trembling from poverty, injustice, and oppression. O Lord, arise, O Father.

O Jehovah, O Commander of the heavenly armies, arise, O Lord, and fulfill Your promises concerning Iran. Lord, remember that it was the Persian magi who were the first to kneel before Your Son, bringing gifts and worshiping Him. Though our history has been taken from us, it was these very Iranians who carried Christianity to China in the sixth century A.D. O Lord, these Iranians have always been devoted to Christ, and You continue to work through them. We come before You, O Lord.

Have mercy on Iran and the Iranian people. Rise up, O Lord, you are the God of justice, the God of salvation, and the God who abhors all evil and injustice. You are the God of love and compassion. Save the people of Iran, save them, O Lord. Those who carry weapons and kill, turn their hearts around, O Lord; lead them to repentance so they may recognize the harm they are

---

[1] (Translator explanation) The phrase "their shadows growing ever longer" is a metaphorical expression. It suggests that the suffering or hardship of the people is increasing over time, and it can symbolize a sense of despair, oppression, or an impending negative outcome. In this context, "shadows" represent the negative forces affecting the people, and "growing ever longer" indicates that these forces are intensifying or lasting longer than expected. It evokes a feeling of ongoing struggle or suffering.

causing. May they lay down their weapons, come to know You, worship You, and praise You.

Father, raise up a worthy leader, a just leader, one who knows You, to save this nation.

In the name of Jesus Christ,

Amen

Amen, dear ones. Let us remain in prayer throughout the day. Our most powerful weapon is prayer, and the Lord has said, "Vengeance and war belong to Me; I will fight for you." The Lord will fight against the forces of darkness, oppression, and injustice.

Amen

# Fifth Day
## Prayer for deliverance from enemies

Today, we continue our prayers for Iran, the Iranian people, and the situation in the country. Through Psalm 28, we lift up our petitions for Iran, all Iranians, and the efforts being made to improve Iran's situation:

*¹To You I will cry, O Lord my Rock: do not be silent to me, lest, if You are silent to me, I become like those who go down to the pit. ²Hear the voice of my supplications when I cry to You, when I lift up my hands toward Your holy sanctuary. ³Do not take me away with the wicked and with the workers of iniquity, who speak peace to their neighbors, but evil is in their hearts. ⁴Give them according to their deeds, and according to the wickedness of their endeavors; give them according to the work of their hands; render to them what they deserve. ⁵Because they do not regard the works of the Lord, nor the operation of His hands, He shall destroy them and not build them up. ⁶Blessed be the Lord, because He has heard the voice of my supplications! ⁷The Lord is my strength and my shield; my heart trusted in Him, and I am helped; therefore, my heart greatly rejoices, and with my song I will praise Him. ⁸The Lord is their strength, and He is the saving refuge of His anointed. ⁹Save Your people, and bless Your inheritance; shepherd them also, and bear them up forever.*

O Father, the people of Iran, Your people, the descendants of those who were the first to come and worship Christ (the Persian Magi), the first to accept Christ as King and Savior and spread Your good news—do not forget them. You are the fortress of salvation for Iran and its people, O Lord. Remove the wicked from this land, O Lord. Turn their hearts, O dear Christ, toward Your love and grace. May those who wield weapons and take lives be ashamed of their actions, turn back, lay down their arms, and embrace Your love.

O Lord, turn them back and transform their hearts. O Jesus Christ, You alone have the power to change hearts. Transform hearts and minds through Your love and healing, Lord Jesus Christ. As You have promised, You will reign over Iran—and You are already reigning. Deliver the people from injustice, suffering, torture, killing, lying, and betrayal, O Lord.

Reign, O Lord, over Iran and its people. Heal the hearts of those who have lost loved ones, or whose loved ones are wounded or imprisoned.

O Lord, awaken this land. Remove the injustice, torture, killing, and these horrendous deeds from Iran and the Iranian people. Save Your people, O Lord. Remember us. We know that You hear our voice, O Lord. Christians from around the world have risen up to pray for Iran. We know that when we pray together, You are with us, You hear us, and You act. Therefore, Lord, we ask for the salvation of Iran and the Iranian people, and we know You are capable of this. Pour out, O Lord, Your Holy Spirit, and save hearts, minds, bodies, and this land.

In the name of Jesus Christ,

Amen

# Sixth Day
## The prayer for God's protection and the future glory of Iran and Iranians

Our devotional today focuses on prayers for our compatriots in Iran and an end to their suffering. Today, the Lord opened my eyes to Isaiah 54, a chapter we read as a divine gift and promise for Iran and its people:

*[1]"Sing, O barren, you who have not borne! Break forth into singing, and cry aloud, you who have not labored with child! For more are the children of the desolate than the children of the married woman," says the Lord.*

(People Worldwide Standing in Support of Iran)

*[2]"Enlarge the place of your tent and let them stretch out the curtains of your dwellings; do not spare; lengthen your cords and strengthen your stakes. [3]For you shall expand to the right and to the left and your descendants will inherit the nations, and make the desolate cities inhabited. [4]"Do not fear, for you will not be ashamed; neither be disgraced, for you will not be put to shame; for you will forget the shame of your youth and will not remember the reproach of your widowhood anymore.*

(Oh Iran)

*[5]For your Maker is your husband; the Lord of hosts is His name; and your Redeemer is the Holy One of Israel; He is called the God of the whole earth. [6]For the Lord has called you like a woman forsaken and grieved in spirit, like a youthful wife when you were refused," says your God. [7]"For a mere moment I have forsaken you, but with great mercies I will gather you. [8]With a little wrath I hid My face from you for a moment; but with everlasting kindness I will have mercy on you," says the Lord, your Redeemer.*

14

*[9]"For this is like the waters of Noah to Me; for as I have sworn that the waters of Noah would no longer cover the earth, so have I sworn that I would not be angry with you, nor rebuke you. [10]For the mountains shall depart, and the hills be removed, but My kindness shall not depart from you, nor shall My covenant of peace be removed," says the Lord, who has mercy on you. [11]"O you afflicted one, tossed with tempest, and not comforted,*

(People of Iran)

*Behold, I will lay your stones with colorful gems and lay your foundations with sapphires. [12]I will make your pinnacles of rubies, Your gates of crystal, and all your walls of precious stones. [13]All your children shall be taught by the Lord, and great shall be the peace of your children. [14]In righteousness you shall be established; You shall be far from oppression, for you shall not fear; and from terror, for it shall not come near you. [15]Indeed they shall surely assemble, but not because of Me. Whoever assembles against you shall fall for your sake. [16]"Behold, I have created the blacksmith who blows the coals in the fire, who brings forth an instrument for his work; and I have created the spoiler to destroy. [17]No weapon formed against you shall prosper, and every tongue which rises against you in judgment You shall condemn. This is the heritage of the servants of the Lord, and their righteousness is from Me," says the Lord.*

Amen

## Seventh Day
## A prayer for the people of Iran

Today, our devotional continues with prayers for Iran and its people, inspired by Psalm 20:

*[1]May the Lord answer you in the day of trouble; may the name of the God of Jacob defend you; [2]may He send you help from the sanctuary and strengthen you out of Zion; [3]may He remember all your offerings and accept your burnt sacrifice. Selah. [4]May He grant you according to your heart's desire and fulfill all your purpose. [5]We will rejoice in your salvation, and in the name of our God we will set up our banners! May the Lord fulfill all your petitions. [6]Now I know that the Lord saves His anointed; He will answer him from His holy heaven with the saving strength of His right hand. [7]Some trust in chariots, and some in horses; but we will remember the name of the Lord our God. [8]They have bowed down and fallen; but we have risen and stand upright. [9]Save, Lord! May the King answer us when we call.*

O Father, You hear our prayers, our cries, and the cries of Iran and its people. You are the God of justice, truth, righteousness, and love. For the people of Iran— for all who suffer under oppression within the country, for those who are imprisoned, and for those grieving the loss of loved ones— Lord, in the name of Jesus Christ, pour out Your peace and comfort upon their hearts. Lift them up, O precious Christ, and pour out Your grace upon them, so that they may come to know You and be filled with Your grace, love, peace, and comfort.

Father, send Your heavenly host of angels to protect the people of Iran. Deliver them from the yoke of oppression, ignorance, superstition, and injustice. Father, You hear our voices; grant us deliverance, O Lord, in the name of Jesus Christ. We pray for all

16

the leaders in Iran who are oppressing the people and causing harm. O Lord, turn their hearts and open their eyes to the truth. Save them, and may they join the people. Bring freedom to this land, to the nation of Iran and Elam, which has long been devoted to You. Send a righteous and capable leader for Iran and its people, and bring an end to this era of oppression, ignorance, and injustice.

In the name of Jesus Christ,

Amen

# Eighth Day
## O Lord, arise and save Iran

Today, as we continue our devotion, we lift our prayers for Iran and its people. Our prayer is drawn from Psalm 3. Let us read this Psalm together, offering it as both a prayer and a declaration of truth over Iran and the Iranian people:

*¹Lord, how they have increased who trouble me! Many are they who rise up against me. ²Many are they who say of me, "there is no help for him in God." Selah. ³But You, O Lord, are a shield for me, my glory and the One who lifts up my head. ⁴I cried to the Lord with my voice, and He heard me from His holy hill. Selah. ⁵I lay down and slept; I awoke, for the Lord sustained me. ⁶I will not be afraid of ten thousands of people who have set themselves against me all around. ⁷Arise, O Lord; save me, O my God! For You have struck all my enemies on the cheekbone; You have broken the teeth of the ungodly. ⁸Salvation belongs to the Lord. Your blessing is upon Your people. Selah.*

O Father, the enemies of Iran and the Iranian people are numerous, and many have risen against them. So many, O Lord, accuse Your people, claiming that they have no place with You. Yet, Lord, You are all-knowing, and You remain the shield and refuge for Iran and its people. You are our glory, O Lord. When we cry out, we know that all Iranians, who are suffering under oppression and injustice, cry out with us. You hear their voices from Your holy hill and answer them.

Thank You, Lord. We praise You, O Jesus Christ, for even in their challenges, they can lay their heads down, sleep, and awaken, assured of Your protection. You are their Protector, and You are ours, because You are Lord. Do not let us fear, even when thousands upon thousands rise up against us and the wicked surround us. Let no fear enter the hearts of Your people, because You are our refuge and strength, O Jesus Christ.

Arise, O Lord! Arise, our God, the God of the Iranian people. Save Iran and its people, because You are the One who fights for them. You are the One who brings the wicked to their knees. You are the One who breaks the power of their oppression.

May those who oppress come to know You, O Jesus Christ, change their ways, lay down their weapons against the people, and join them in unity. O Lord, put an end to injustice, wickedness, and murder in Iran once and for all.

Free the people and the land of Iran so they may worship You freely, O Jesus Christ, and live in the freedom, peace, tranquility, and rest that You give.

O Lord, Your people are in need of Your peace and comfort, O Jesus Christ. Pour out Your Holy Spirit, the Spirit of peace and comfort, upon them. Save them, Father. Save them. Save them.

In the name of Jesus Christ,

Amen

# Ninth Day
## Father, You are the way and the truth for the righteous

As we continue to lift our prayers for Iran and its people during this critical time, today's devotional draws inspiration from Psalm 1:

*¹Blessed is the man who walks not in the counsel of the ungodly, nor stands in the path of sinners, nor sits in the seat of the scornful; ²But his delight is in the law of the Lord, and in His law, he meditates day and night. ³He shall be like a tree planted by the rivers of water, that brings forth its fruit in its season, whose leaf also shall not wither; and whatever he does shall prosper. ⁴The ungodly are not so but are like the chaff which the wind drives away. ⁵Therefore the ungodly shall not stand in the judgment, nor sinners in the congregation of the righteous. ⁶For the Lord knows the way of the righteous, but the way of the ungodly shall perish.*

Amen

O Father, we thank You for Your boundless love and compassion, which extend from earth to heaven. We are grateful, O Lord, that even when we were Your enemies, You did not withhold Your Son from us. Thank You, O Jesus Christ, for shedding Your blood on the cross, by which You redeemed us from our sins, and for rising on the third day, and freeing us from bondage.

And thank You, precious Holy Spirit, for dwelling within us when we accept Jesus Christ as our Savior and Lord.

O Lord, we bring before You the situation of Iran and its people. You, Father, are fully aware of all things. Your Word declares that the wicked cannot stand before You; they are like chaff that the wind blows away, and You will destroy their ways, while You will always uplift the righteous. O Lord, have mercy on the people of Iran and upon this nation. Father, take their hands, reveal Your great light in Jesus Christ to each one, and save them, O Lord, both in spirit and in body.

O Lord, remove all evil, oppression, anger, hatred, murder, and persecution from Iran and its people. Reign in the hearts of all, including ours, with Your love and compassion. You are able, O Lord, to save. Heal the broken-hearted, bind up the grieving souls, and bring an end to oppression and injustice.

Today, we place Iran and its people into Your holy hands. We declare, O Lord, deliver them spiritually and physically, and reign over Iran with Your love, compassion, and grace, O Jesus Christ.

In the name of Jesus Christ,

Amen

# Tenth Day
## The Lord is able to bring to completion the great work He has begun in the people of Iran

Today's devotion is from Philippians 1:3-12. Let us come together in prayer for Iran, its people, and the trials and hardships they are enduring:

*³I thank my God upon every remembrance of you, ⁴always in every prayer of mine making request for you all with joy,*

I pray with joy, trusting that the work that has begun—by God's will—will bring an end to persecution, oppression, and injustice.

*⁵For your fellowship in the gospel from the first day until now, ⁶being confident of this very thing, that He who has begun a good work in you will complete it until the day of Jesus Christ.*

The Lord's works are great, and He always fulfills His promises. He is able to complete the work He has begun in each of us as Christians and in all Iranians.

*⁷Just as it is right for me to think this of you all, because I have you in my heart, inasmuch as both in my chains and in the defense and confirmation of the gospel, you all are partakers with me of grace. ⁸For God is my witness, how greatly I long for you all with the affection of Jesus Christ. ⁹And this I pray that your love may abound still more and more in knowledge and all discernment,*

So that your love for one another, for Iran, for the Iranian people, and even for your enemies—the evildoers and those who take up arms against Iranians—may increase.

*¹⁰that you may approve the things that are excellent,*

My prayer for the Iranian people and for this situation is that they may have the best discernment.

*that you may be sincere and without offense till the day of Christ.*

Our desire is that the Lord Jesus Christ may touch each Iranian, embracing them with His love, grace, goodness, and protection.

*[11] Being filled with the fruits of righteousness which are by Jesus Christ, to the glory and praise of God.*

O Father, we trust that You are fully aware of all that is unfolding, and that You will use it all for the glory of Your name. Lord, hear the cry of the people of Iran. O Jesus Christ, reveal Yourself to them. Grant them love, compassion, and grace. Protect them from the wicked, O Lord. Give them wisdom to know where to go, where not to go, what to say, and what not to say.

And, O Lord, turn even the wicked and our enemies towards You, so that they may come to know You, O Jesus Christ, and experience freedom in You. And, Lord, remove the injustice, the executions, and the suffering and torture from our people.

Lord, we bring before You those who are in prison. O Lord, O Jesus Christ, protect them and bring them out safely and unharmed. We also bring before You the jailers and all the authorities, that You may transform their hearts and open their eyes to the truth, so they may recognize what they are doing. May they lay down their weapons, turn to the people, join You, O Jesus Christ, and find freedom in You. Lord, we thank You for Your goodness and kindness. Lift up the people of Iran and bring them to know You. Raise up a good leader, one whose heart beats for You, O Father, to lead the people and bring an end to the works of the wicked in Iran.

In the name of Jesus Christ,

Amen

## Eleventh Day
## The Lord has heard the voice of our cries and pleas

Our devotional today is from Psalm 116, which we offer as a prayer and heartfelt appeal to God for Iran, the Iranian people, and ourselves—especially in regard to the situation in Iran and Iranian people:

*¹I love the Lord, because He has heard my voice and my supplications. ²Because He has inclined His ear to me; therefore, I will call upon Him as long as I live. ³The pains of death surrounded me and the pangs of Sheol laid hold of me; I found trouble and sorrow. ⁴Then I called upon the name of the Lord: "O Lord, I implore You, deliver my soul!" ⁵Gracious is the Lord and righteous; yes, our God is merciful.*

Our God, the God of the Father and Jesus Christ, is compassionate.

*⁶The Lord preserves the simple; I was brought low and He saved me. ⁷Return to your rest, O my soul, for the Lord has dealt bountifully with you. ⁸For You have delivered my soul from death, my eyes from tears, and my feet from falling. ⁹I will walk before the Lord in the land of the living.¹⁰I believed, therefore I spoke, "I am greatly afflicted."¹¹I said in my haste, "all men are liars." ¹²What shall I render to the Lord for all His benefits toward me?¹³I will take up the cup of salvation and call upon the name of the Lord. ¹⁴I will pay my vows to the Lord, now in the presence of all His people. ¹⁵Precious in the sight of the Lord; is the death of His saints.¹⁶O Lord, truly I am Your servant; I am Your servant, the son of Your maidservant; You have loosed my bonds. ¹⁷I will offer to You the sacrifice of thanksgiving and will call upon the name of the Lord. ¹⁸ I will pay my vows to the Lord, now in the presence of all His people, ¹⁹in the courts of the Lord's house, in the midst of you, O Jerusalem.*

Hallelujah, hallelujah, hallelujah.

Yes, Lord. In times of hardship and distress, Father, when we come to You— Jesus Christ—You say, "Come to Me, all who are burdened; lay down your burdens and take Mine instead, because I am gentle and humble and I will give you rest—not as the world gives, but the peace that comes from Me. Jesus Christ, pour out Your peace, love, and grace upon Iran and all Iranians who are enduring suffering and persecution.

O Lord, You have said that when we lift our voices to You and call upon Your name—the name of Jesus Christ, which, as Philippians declares, is above every name—every tongue will confess that Jesus Christ is Lord, and every knee will bow before Him.

Jesus Christ, we call upon Your name. You have promised that whatever we ask in Your name will be given to us. So, in Your name, we come before the Father. In the name of Jesus Christ, Lord, rescue Iran and its people from death. Deliver them from oppression. We know that You are able, and we ask You to act. Lord, protect each person who has suffered and those who are imprisoned. Grant them freedom, O Lord.

Lord, turn the hearts of the wicked, transform them, and change their course so that they may come to know You, O Jesus Christ, and cease their evil ways. Raise up the nation of Iran, which was once a symbol of faith in You, O Jesus Christ—and still remains. Deliver it, and establish Your throne, O Father, upon Iran and reign. Be with all those who mourn, with all those who are suffering, O Lord, and as David writes, save their souls. Remove this wickedness, injustice, oppression, and bloodshed swiftly, and pour Your freedom upon Iran.

In the name of Jesus Christ,

Amen

## Twelfth Day
## O Lord, hear us and answer our prayer

Our devotional today is from Psalm 86, which we offer as a prayer for Iran and Iranian people:

*¹Bow down Your ear, O Lord, hear me; for I am poor and needy. ²Preserve my life, for I am holy; You are my God; save Your servant who trusts in You! ³ Be merciful to me, O Lord, for I cry to You all day long.*

Grant grace to Iran and the Iranian people, O Lord.

*⁴Rejoice the soul of Your servant, Lord, for to You, O Lord, I lift up my soul. ⁵For You, Lord, are good and ready to forgive, and abundant in mercy to all those who call upon You.*

So, O people of Iran, O Iranians, call upon the name of the Lord—the name of the Father and of Jesus Christ, which is above all names.

*⁶Give ear, O Lord, to my prayer; and attend to the voice of my supplications. ⁷In the day of my trouble I will call upon You, for You will answer me.*

Father, we come before You and ask: Heal Iran and the Iranian people, O Lord. Holy Spirit, pour out upon Iran and its people and grant them salvation, O Lord. Father, restrain the hands of the wicked. Even turn the wicked back, O Lord. Turn the wicked back, O Lord. Touch their hearts and turn them toward You. Father, save Your land—Elam. Save the people of Iran, O Lord. Heal the broken-hearted, O God. You are the hope of the poor and oppressed. Father, in the name of Jesus Christ, we lift up those who are in prison. Those who have been imprisoned—O Lord, protect them in the name of Jesus Christ. Guard them and bring them out safe and sound.

Lord, transform the hearts of the prison guards and lead them toward You, toward love, and toward goodness. Rescue these people from oppression, injustice, and suffering, and bring freedom to Iran, O Lord. As You stated in Jeremiah 49, establish Your throne over Iran and reign, O Jesus Christ. With humility, we come before You and say: Father, only You can accomplish all of this, and we trust that You have heard our voices and will bring it to pass.

In the name of Jesus Christ,

Amen

# Thirteenth Day
## Thanksgiving

Today is a day of thanksgiving. We gather to come before the Lord and express our gratitude for His blessings and the great things He has done for us. The Word of the Lord tells us, with thanksgiving, we come before You, O Father; with thanksgiving, we come before You, O Jesus Christ. So, let us lift our voices today and give thanks to the Lord for all His blessings, goodness, and love.

Father, we thank You for not withholding Your precious Son from us when we were Your enemies, knowing that we could not attain Your holiness through our own efforts. From the very beginning, You established and fulfilled Your plan. You sent Your Son to shed His blood on the cross for each of us, offering the complete sacrifice for the sins of humanity—those who were, are, and will be. So that, through the shedding of the Lord's blood, there would be no limitation to salvation. One blood, one sacrifice, and once and for all, through Jesus Christ. Thank you, Jesus Christ our Lord, for going to the cross for us when we were Your enemies. You died for our sins and curses, Your blood was shed, and with Your blood, You washed away all our sins and curses. Thank you, Jesus Christ, for rising from the dead on the third day, conquering death and Satan, and reconciling us with the Father.

Now, we can come to You with ease, call upon Your name, lift You up, and say, "Father," because You have not given us a spirit of fear. Thank You, Lord, for removing the spirit of fear, worry, confusion, and anxiety from us. You tell us, "I have not given you a spirit of fear, but a spirit of adoption, so that you may call Me 'Daddy 'and 'Abba.'" Thank You, Lord, for Your Holy Spirit. Thank You, dear Holy Spirit, for dwelling in the hearts of each one of us who has chosen Jesus Christ as Lord, Leader, Savior, and

Redeemer. Holy Spirit, reign in each of us. Fill us, Lord, overflow us, and remove anything that is not Yours, replacing it with Yourself.

Thank You, Lord, for making us the salt and light of this world. Thank You, Lord, that we can come before You without fear or worry, calling upon You wherever we are and in every circumstance. Thank You that as Your Word says, *"All things will work together for the good of those who are called by Your name."* And thank You for declaring that no weapon formed against us will prosper, and for the promise that when the Lord is with us, no one can stand against us. All of Your promises are true, from the beginning to eternity. So, we are grateful to You.

Thank You, Lord, for all that You do in each of our lives. Thank You for the storms, the challenges, and the lessons You have taught us. Lord, open our eyes so we can see Your blessings and always offer our gratitude to You. Thank You, Father, You are the beginning and the end, the first and the last; You are the foundation and the purpose of our lives. May our light shine brightly, and may Your Holy Spirit bear fruit within us, so that others will see and come to worship You. Thank You for our lives, for our salvation, for our families, for healing, and for the work You have started and continue to do in Iran, which You will bring to completion.

Thank you, Lord, that your work has begun in Iran—the work of cleansing, the work of removing evil, crime, and injustice, because you do not love injustice. You, Lord, are a God of love, justice, peace, and tranquility. So, dear Holy Spirit, pour out your purity, your peace, and your harmony upon Iran. Lift up the oppressed, the wronged, and those in mourning, Lord, and bring each of them to know you. Bring the enemies and the wicked as well, so that they may come to know you, Jesus Christ, lay down their weapons and actions, and embrace love, kindness, and justice.

We bring the prisoners before You today, Lord. In the name of Jesus Christ, our Lord, free each one of them and bring them out. Do not let any harm come to them, Lord. You are capable, Father. Lord, save and protect the prisoners, and we thank You, Father, that You will bring this work to completion for Iran and the Iranian people.

And You, Jesus Christ, as stated in Jeremiah 49:38, reign over Iran and the Iranian people, for Your reign is one of love and compassion. While kings take life to become rulers of this world, our King, Jesus Christ, gave His life to become the King of hearts. Reign, Jesus Christ. We thank You for being such a loving and compassionate King.

In the name of Jesus Christ,

Amen

# Fourteenth Day
## O God, our righteous defender, answer our plea

Our devotional today comes from Psalm 4, and we continue to lift our prayers for Iran and its people. Let us present this psalm before the Lord as a prayer and petition, trusting that He is faithful to complete the work He has begun:

*¹Hear me when I call, O God of my righteousness! You have relieved me in my distress; have mercy on me and hear my prayer. ²How long, O you sons of men, will you turn my glory to shame? How long will you love worthlessness and seek falsehood? Selah. ³But know that the Lord has set apart for Himself him who is godly. The Lord will hear when I call to Him. ⁴Be angry and do not sin. Meditate within your heart on your bed and be still. Selah. ⁵Offer the sacrifices of righteousness and put your trust in the Lord. ⁶There are many who say, "who will show us any good?" Lord, lift up the light of Your countenance upon us. ⁷You have put gladness in my heart, more than in the season that their grain and wine increased. ⁸I will both lie down in peace and sleep; for You alone, O Lord, make me dwell in safety.*

Amen. We come before our righteous God, confident that when we call upon Him, He hears and answers our prayers. Lord, hear our prayer for Iran and its people. Rise up, Lord, and deliver the nation and its people from oppression, injustice, ignorance, and persecution. Bring down those who pursue deception and falsehood.

And Lord, You have set apart and lifted up those who are devoted to You, granting them peace. Lord, pour Your peace upon the people of Iran—upon the grieving, the mourning, and those in prison. Comfort the mothers, fathers, brothers, and sisters who have lost their loved ones. Jesus Christ, You are the One who

31

shows mercy. Shine the light of Your face upon Iran and its people. Jesus Christ, the Light of the world and the Living Water, bring salvation to Iran, Lord.

Set the people free, O Father, and bring them to recognize You as Lord, as their Savior, Jesus Christ, so they may experience Your grace and love. Grain, new wine, and such things do not bring us peace, for true peace and well-being come only from You, O Lord. Therefore, grant this peace, calm, and tranquility to Iran and its people, O Lord.

O Father, complete the great work You have begun in Iran without any bloodshed, bringing it to fulfillment and perfection, O Lord. Free the prisoners, Lord, and release each one of them. Protect them, O Lord.

Have mercy on the oppressors and transform their hearts so that they, too, may come to know You and embrace love, not cruelty and injustice, O Father. We place Iran and its people in Your loving, blessed, and righteous hands, O Father. Finish the work You have started.

In the name of Jesus Christ,

Amen

# Fifteenth Day
## In the Name of the Lord, we will destroy our enemies

Our devotional today is based on Psalm 118:5-15, and we continue it as a prayer for Iran, the Iranian people, and the challenges Iran and its people are facing:

*⁵I called on the Lord in distress; the Lord answered me and set me in a broad place. ⁶The Lord is on my side; I will not fear. What can man do to me? ⁷The Lord is for me among those who help me; therefore, I shall see my desire on those who hate me. ⁸It is better to trust in the Lord, than to put confidence in man. ⁹It is better to trust in the Lord, than to put confidence in princes. ¹⁰All nations surrounded me, but in the name of the Lord I will destroy them. ¹¹They surrounded me, yes, they surrounded me; but in the name of the Lord I will destroy them. ¹²They surrounded me like bees. They were quenched like a fire of thorns. For in the name of the Lord I will destroy them. ¹³You pushed me violently, that I might fall, but the Lord helped me. ¹⁴The Lord is my strength and song, and He has become my salvation. ¹⁵The voice of rejoicing and salvation is in the tents of the righteous; the right hand of the Lord does valiantly.*

Amen

O Lord, in times of distress, Iran and the Iranian people call upon Your name, O Jesus Christ. You are the One who answers us. You are the One who responds to the Iranians and grants them relief. Lord, You are with the Iranians and with us. Therefore, O Lord, we will not fear. You are the strength and support of Iran and the Iranian people. You, O Lord, are the One to whom we and all the Iranians turn for refuge. May the eyes of the Iranians be opened, and O Jesus Christ, may they see You as their Savior, Life, Refuge, and Stronghold—turning to You and seeking everything from You. You are the One who is capable; You are the One to whom we must turn—not to man or rulers, but only to the Lord, for You, O Lord, are the greatest, the strongest, the best, and the most compassionate, O Lord.

When all the nations surround Iran and its people, it is only in Your name, O Lord—when we call upon Your name—they will vanish and be destroyed. In Your name, O Jesus Christ, the name that is above every name, every knee will bow, and every tongue will confess that You are Lord.

Even if they surround us like bees—encircling Iran and its people, stinging like bees— Your word says, O Lord, that when we call on Your name, they will be extinguished like a fire quickly burning out among the thorns, and they will disappear and be no more.

Therefore, O Lord, in Your name, O Jesus Christ, we rise and declare: Lord, put an end to the evil of the wicked, the oppressors, and those who have surrounded Iran and its people to consume and destroy them. Pour out Your freedom, justice, love, peace, and tranquility upon Iran and its people, O Lord, and bring to completion the work You have begun. O Father, we place Iran, its people, and this entire situation in Your gracious and loving hands, knowing that You are able to bring victory and joy to the homes and the nation of Iran.

In the name of Jesus Christ,

Amen

# Sixteenth Day
## Jesus Christ, arise and show compassion to Iranians

Today, our devotional comes from Psalm 102, and we present it before the Lord as the heartfelt cry of our hearts, of Iran, and its people. As we read, wherever it says "I" or "Zion," we replace it with Iran and the Iranian people:

*[1]Hear my prayer, O Lord, and let my cry come to You. [2]Do not hide Your face from me in the day of my trouble; incline Your ear to me. In the day that I call, answer me speedily. [3]For my days are consumed like smoke, and my bones are burned like a hearth. [4]My heart is stricken and withered like grass, so that I forget to eat my bread. [5]Because of the sound of my groaning, my bones cling to my skin. [6]I am like a pelican of the wilderness. I am like an owl of the desert. [7]I lie awake and am like a sparrow alone on the housetop. [8]My enemies reproach me all day long; those who deride me swear an oath against me. [9]For I have eaten ashes like bread and mingled my drink with weeping. [10]Because of Your indignation and Your wrath; for You have lifted me up and cast me away. [11]My days are like a shadow that lengthens, and I wither away like grass. [12]But You, O Lord, shall endure forever, and the remembrance of Your name to all generations. [13]You will arise and have mercy on Zion; for the time to favor her, yes, the set time, has come.*

Yes, O Lord, the time has come for You to look upon Iran with favor.

*[14]For Your servants take pleasure in her stones and show favor to her dust. [15]So the nations shall fear the name of the Lord,*

Yes, O Lord, the nations shall fear Your name, O Father.

35

*And all the kings of the earth Your glory. ¹⁶For the Lord shall build up Zion; He shall appear in His glory.*

Because the Lord will establish Iran.

*¹⁷He shall regard the prayer of the destitute and shall not despise their prayer. ¹⁸This will be written for the generation to come, that a people yet to be created may praise the Lord. ¹⁹For He looked down from the height of His sanctuary; from heaven the Lord viewed the earth,*

He looked upon the earth, upon Iran.

*²⁰To hear the groaning of the prisoner, to release those appointed to death, ²¹To declare the name of the Lord in Zion and His praise in Jerusalem,*

To declare the name of Jesus Christ throughout all of Iran.

*²²When the peoples are gathered together and the kingdoms to serve the Lord.*

Amen. Amen, O Lord

Lord, look upon Iran—its people, the oppressed, the mourners, the poor, the hungry, and the thirsty—with Your mercy. You have heard our cry. Come, O Lord, look upon the captives and the people of Iran, and free them from injustice, cruelty, ignorance, superstition, slaughter, wrath, and hatred, O Jesus Christ. Reign over Iran and its people, O Lord. May Iran become the first Christian nation in the Middle East, so it can experience Your grace, love, and mercy every day. Thank You, O Father.

In the name of Jesus Christ,

Amen

## Seventeenth Day
## The Lord is good

Our devotional today is drawn from Psalm 118:17-29. We offer these verses as a prayer before the Lord for the situation in Iran, for our beloved compatriots, and for those enduring oppression and persecution, that it may be a source of hope for each of us:

*[17] I shall not die, but live, and declare the works of the Lord.*

Iran and the Iranian people shall not die but live and declare the works of the Lord. And we will all declare the works of the Lord.

*[18] The Lord has chastened me severely, but He has not given me over to death.*

The Lord has not abandoned Iran and its people to death.

*[19] Open to me the gates of righteousness; I will go through them and I will praise the Lord. [20] This is the gate of the Lord, through which the righteous shall enter. [21] I will praise You, for You have answered me and have become my salvation.*

You have become the salvation of Iran and its people, O Lord.

*[22] The stone which the builders rejected has become the chief cornerstone. [23] This was the Lord's doing; it is marvelous in our eyes. [24] This is the day the Lord has made; we will rejoice and be glad in it.*

Yes, Lord, this is the day You have made; we will rejoice and be glad in it.

*[25] Save now, I pray, O Lord; O Lord, I pray, send now prosperity.*

O Lord, send prosperity to Iran and its people.

*$^{26}$Blessed is he who comes in the name of the Lord! We have blessed you from the house of the Lord. $^{27}$God is the Lord and He has given us light; bind the sacrifice with cords to the horns of the altar. $^{28}$You are my God, and I will praise You; You are my God, I will exalt You. $^{29}$Oh, give thanks to the Lord, for He is good! For His mercy endures forever.*

Yes, O Father, You are good. Your mercy endures forever.

And Your love for the Iranians, those who were the first to come, knelt before Your Son, brought Him gifts, and acknowledged Him as King and Savior. Iranians whom You have not forgotten. Iranians whom You used to deliver Your people, Israel, and restore them to the temple.

The Iranians You promised, O Lord, that in the last days, You will establish Your throne upon Elam, gather all Iranians from every corner, and scatter all rulers. But in those days, You will restore the glory of Iran. We trust and know, O Lord, that Your promises are great, and the cornerstone, Jesus Christ the Lord, will be the foundation of a new Iran.

Father, fulfill Your work in Iran. Save Iranians who are enduring hardship, be with them, and protect them. Put an end to the violence and hatred, Father. Lord, grant peace, tranquility, and serenity to Iran and its people in the name of Jesus Christ, and reign over Iran and its people. May Iran become the first Christian nation in the Middle East, and may Your love, glory, grace, and mercy flow from it to the world.

In the name of Jesus Christ, our Lord,

Amen

# Eighteenth Day
## Prayer for the prisoners in the fire

Father, we are hearing distressing news from Iran. We have just learned that Evin Prison has been set on fire. O Lord, we don't know how or why this happened. But, Lord, we come before You, O Jesus Christ. We pray, Father, in Your glorious name, have mercy on Iran and its people. Have mercy on the prisoners in this prison, O Lord, and bring each one of them safely out of the fire.

Father, use this situation, because everything works for the good of those who love You. You have promised that all things will work together for the good of those who love You, Father. Use this, Father, to bring an end to the crimes, injustices, and oppression in Iran. Lord, may Your loving hand, O Jesus Christ, be upon Iran. May every Iranian come to know You, because You are the Lord of love, compassion, and peace.

Pour Your love, compassion, well-being, peace, and tranquility upon Iran and its people, O Lord. Bless the hearts of those who are now distressed, O Lord. Protect them and lift them up, O Lord, in the name of Jesus Christ. And Father, save them all. Save Iran.

May Iran become the first Christian nation in the Middle East, Father. Do Your work. Reign in Iran, and save the people. Put an end to these crimes, killings, and injustices, O Lord.

We pray in the name of Jesus Christ, our Lord, and receive with faith.

Amen

# Nineteenth Day
## But we will call on the name of Jehovah

Our devotional today is based on Psalm 20 and serves as a prayer for Iran, its people, and the current situation in Iran. Together, we turn to the Lord and pray this psalm for Iran and for the Iranians who are suffering under oppression:

*¹May the Lord answer you in the day of trouble; May the name of the God of Jacob defend you;*

O Iran and Iranians,

*²May He send you help from the sanctuary and strengthen you out of Zion; ³May He remember all your offerings and accept your burnt sacrifice. Selah. ⁴May He grant you according to your heart's desire and fulfill all your purpose. ⁵We will rejoice in your salvation and in the name of our God we will set up our banners! May the Lord fulfill all your petitions.*

O Iran and Iranians,

*⁶Now I know that the Lord saves His anointed;*

Now I know that the Lord will save His Iran and its people.

*He will answer him from His holy heaven with the saving strength of His right hand. ⁷Some trust in chariots and some in horses; but we will remember the name of the Lord our God. ⁸They have bowed down and fallen; but we have risen and stand upright.*

And we, the Iranian people, will rise and stand upright.

*⁹Save, Lord! May the King answer us when we call.*

O Lord, save Iran.

Amen

Father, we ask You to accept this prayer from us for Iran and the Iranian people. We know that You are present, and we know, O Father, that You are deeply grieved by the oppression, injustice, cruelty, pride, arrogance, and the bloodshed that brings despair. Your heart is filled with sorrow.

Lord, You hear the voices of each one of us—every father and mother who grieves in Iran, all those who suffer under oppression, and the prisoners whose whereabouts and conditions are unknown. Lord, You are aware of everything, O Father, and Your heart bears the greatest sorrow of all.

O dear Christ, reveal Yourself to Iran and the Iranian people with Your love and grace. Lord, set Iran and its people free. Place Your throne over Iran and the Iranians, and turn the hearts of the oppressors and wrongdoers, so that they too may come to know You, O Jesus Christ, and cease their torment, oppression, cruelty, and injustice against the people.

Father, bring to completion the work You have begun in Iran, and remove oppression, injustice, and the oppressors from this land and its people, O Lord. Father, Iran is in Your hands, and the Iranians are in Your hands. Father, may Iran become the first Christian nation in the Middle East. Save us, O Lord, and reign over Iran with love and compassion.

In the name of Jesus Christ,

Amen

# Twentieth Day
## Lord, hide the Iranians under Your wings

Our devotional today is from Psalm 17:6-15, and with this psalm, we continue our prayer for Iran, its situation, and its people, both in Iran and abroad:

*6I have called upon You, for You will hear me, O God; incline Your ear to me and hear my speech. 7Show Your marvelous lovingkindness by Your right hand, O You who save those who trust in You, from those who rise up against them. 8Keep me as the apple of Your eye; hide me under the shadow of Your wings, 9from the wicked who oppress me, from my deadly enemies who surround me.*

Yes, Lord, hide Iran and its people under Your wings. Protect them from the wicked who seek their destruction, and from their enemies who have surrounded them. Guard them as the apple of Your eye.

*10They have closed up their fat hearts; with their mouths they speak proudly. 11They have now surrounded us in our steps; they have set their eyes, crouching down to the earth, 12as a lion is eager to tear his prey, and like a young lion lurking in secret places. 13Arise, O Lord, confront him, cast him down; deliver my life from the wicked with Your sword,*

Deliver the soul of Iran and its people, O Lord.

*14With Your hand from men, O Lord, from men of the world who have their portion in this life, and whose belly You fill with Your hidden treasure. They are satisfied with children and leave the rest of their possession for their babes. 15As for me, I will see Your face in righteousness; I shall be satisfied when I awake in Your likeness.*

Yes, O Lord, we thank You, Father, for hearing our voices—the voices of Iranians and the voice of Iran. We know that Your love reaches from the earth to the heavens, Father. Thank You, Holy Spirit, for revealing Your mysteries to each of us—the mystery of salvation, O Lord, fulfilled in the last days through Your Son, Jesus Christ. Through His death on the cross and His blood shed for the sins of all people, He rose on the third day, conquering death and defeating Satan. He has been given a name above every name, in heaven, on earth, and beneath the earth.

In this name—the name of Jesus Christ—we come before You. In this powerful name, we rebuke the forces of darkness. In this name, we stand upright, and in this name, we pray, because, Jesus, You have promised, *"Whatever you ask in My name, the Father will give you."*

So, Father, in the name of Jesus Christ, we entrust Iran and the Iranian people into Your blessed, loving and mighty hands. Protect every one of them, Lord. Deliver them from oppressors and tyrants, Lord, and hide them under Your wings.

Lord, bring an end to this persecution, oppression, violence, and bloodshed. Reign over Iran and its people, O Jesus Christ, because Your yoke is easy and Your burden is light, because You are humble and gentle. May all the people of Iran come to know You, including those who oppress and persecute—may they turn their hearts to You and find salvation. Save Iran and its people, Lord, and establish Your reign over the nation.

In the name of Jesus Christ,

Amen

# Twenty-First Day
## Our shield Is the Lord

Our devotional today continues as a prayer for Iran and the Iranian people. We are praying from Psalm 7. Together, we read Psalm 7 as a prayer for Iran, its people, and for ourselves:

*[1] O Lord my God, in You I put my trust; save me from all those who persecute me; and deliver me,*

O Lord, deliver Iran and the Iranians, who are in darkness, from all their pursuers and set them free.

*[2] Lest they tear me like a lion, rending me in pieces, while there is none to deliver.*

Lest, O Lord, they tear apart Iran and the Iranians like lions, with no one to rescue them.

*[3] O Lord my God, if I have done this: if there is iniquity in my hands, [4] if I have repaid evil to him, who was at peace with me or have plundered my enemy without cause. [5] Let the enemy pursue me and overtake me; yes, let him trample my life to the earth and lay my honor in the dust. Selah. [6] Arise, O Lord, in Your anger; lift Yourself up because of the rage of my enemies; rise up for me to the judgment You have commanded!*

Arise for us, the Iranians.

*[7] So the congregation of the peoples shall surround You; for their sakes, therefore, return on high. [8] The Lord shall judge the peoples; Judge me, O Lord, according to my righteousness and according to my integrity within me. [9] Oh, let the wickedness of the wicked come to an end, but establish the just; for the righteous God tests the hearts and minds. [10] My defense is of God, who saves the upright in heart. [11] God is a just judge and God is angry with the wicked every day. [12] If he does not turn back; He will sharpen His*

*sword; He bends His bow and makes it ready.* <sup>13</sup>*He also prepares for Himself instruments of death. He makes His arrows into fiery shafts.* <sup>14</sup>*Behold, the wicked brings forth iniquity; Yes, he conceives trouble and brings forth falsehood.* <sup>15</sup>*He made a pit and dug it out and has fallen into the ditch which he made.* <sup>16</sup>*His trouble shall return upon his own head and his violent dealing shall come down on his own crown.* <sup>17</sup>*I will praise the Lord according to His righteousness and will sing praise to the name of the Lord Most High.*

Amen.

Father, O righteous Lord, O Lord full of love, O great and powerful Lord, vengeance belongs to You. Fight for Iran and the Iranians, O Lord, and allow them to stand and witness—let all see that You are the Lord. You are the Father who loved us so much that, even when we were Your enemies, You did not withhold Your Son from us, and You remain the same God.

O Jesus Christ, pour out Your love, compassion, and grace upon Iran and the Iranians and deliver them. Deliver them, O Lord; deliver them spiritually and physically. Remove the wicked and the evil ones from Iran and the Iranians, O Lord. Transform their hearts, so that they too may come to know You, O Jesus Christ, be saved, and leave behind conflict, oppression, and evil, choosing love as their way.

O Lord, may Iran become the first Christian nation in the Middle East, able to show Your love and compassion to all. We pray this in the name of Jesus Christ, our Lord,

Amen

# Twenty-Second Day
## God Is the strength of our hearts

Today, we continue our devotional time with prayer for Iran, Iranians, and our fellow countrymen, guided by Psalm 73.

This psalm is especially meaningful because, at times, when we see those who do not believe in God seemingly enjoying comfort, prosperity, and peace, we may find ourselves struggling with envy. Yet, this psalm offers deep insight, making it particularly relevant to Iran's circumstances and the challenges we and our fellow countrymen face.

Let us read it together:

*¹Truly God is good to Israel, to such as are pure in heart.*

God is good to Iran.

*²But as for me, my feet had almost stumbled; my steps had nearly slipped. ³For I was envious of the boastful, when I saw the prosperity of the wicked. ⁴For there are no pangs in their death, but their strength is firm. ⁵They are not in trouble as other men, nor are they plagued like other men. ⁶Therefore pride serves as their necklace; violence covers them like a garment. ⁷Their eyes bulge with abundance; they have more than heart could wish. ⁸They scoff and speak wickedly concerning oppression; they speak loftily. ⁹They set their mouth against the heavens, and their tongue walks through the earth. ¹⁰Therefore his people return here, and waters of a full cup are drained by them. ¹¹And they say, "How does God know? and is there knowledge in the Most High?"¹²Behold, these are the ungodly, who are always at ease; they increase in riches. ¹³Surely I have cleansed my heart in vain and washed my hands in innocence. ¹⁴For all day long I have been plagued and chastened every morning. ¹⁵If I had said, "I will speak thus," behold, I would have been untrue to the generation of Your children. ¹⁶When I thought how to understand this, it was too painful for me— ¹⁷until I went into the sanctuary of God; then I understood their end. ¹⁸Surely You set them in slippery places. You cast them down to destruction. ¹⁹Oh, how they are brought to desolation as in a moment! They are utterly consumed with terrors. ²⁰As a dream when one awakes, so, Lord, when You awake, you shall despise their image. ²¹Thus my heart was grieved, and I was vexed in my mind. ²²I was so foolish and ignorant; I was like a beast before You. ²³Nevertheless I am continually with You; You hold me by my right hand.*

*²⁴You will guide me with Your counsel and afterward receive me to glory. ²⁵Whom have I in heaven but You? And there is none upon earth that I desire besides You. ²⁶My flesh and my heart fail; but God is the strength of my heart and my portion forever. ²⁷For indeed, those who are far from You shall perish; You have destroyed all those who desert You for harlotry. ²⁸But it is good for me to draw near to God; I have put my trust in the Lord God, that I may declare all Your works.*

Amen

Dear friends, the Lord reminds us that while the wicked may seem full of pride, free from illness, increasing in wealth, and speaking with arrogance and violence as if everything belongs to them, the truth is that He humbles the proud and stands with those who are pure in heart.

The Lord sees all the actions of the wicked, who speak in this manner. They are like a fleeting dream—here today, gone tomorrow, leaving no trace behind. Therefore, let us therefore remain pure in heart and walk with the Lord Jesus Christ. His Word assures us that nothing, not even storms or hardships, can separate us from His love.

The fate of all the oppressors, the wicked, the wrongdoers, and the arrogant who rule over Iran and oppress its people is clear according to God's Word. For this reason, we pray for them as well: Lord, have mercy on them. Open their eyes so they may see the truth. Save them, so they may come to know You, Jesus Christ, as Lord and Master, and follow You.

In the name of Jesus Christ,

Amen

# Twenty-Third Day
## We place our trust in God's love

Today, our devotional comes from Psalm 52, and through it, we continue our prayer for the situation in Iran and for our fellow countrymen:

*¹Why do you boast in evil, O mighty man? The goodness of God endures continually. ²Your tongue devises destruction, like a sharp razor, working deceitfully. ³You love evil more than good, lying rather than speaking righteousness. Selah. ⁴You love all devouring words, your deceitful tongue. ⁵God shall likewise destroy you forever; He shall take you away and pluck you out of your dwelling place and uproot you from the land of the living. Selah. ⁶The righteous also shall see and fear and shall laugh at him, saying, ⁷"here is the man who did not make God his strength, but trusted in the abundance of his riches and strengthened himself in his wickedness." ⁸But I am like a green olive tree in the house of God; I trust in the mercy of God forever and ever. ⁹I will praise You forever, because You have done it; and in the presence of Your saints I will wait on Your name, for it is good.*

Amen. Father, we thank You and are grateful for all the goodness, blessings, and for everything You have done and continue to do. O Lord, Your Word says that the wicked, the oppressors, the deceivers, and the liars will not remain on this earth, and You will remove them. The righteous will remain and witness how the oppressors, deceivers, and liars will perish. And You will reign, O Lord.

So, O Lord, intervene for the people of Iran and for Iran. Complete the great work You began in Iran, O Father. O Jesus Christ, we bring the deceivers, the liars, and the oppressors before You as well; O Lord, save them too. They need You, O Jesus

Christ, more than anyone else. Open their eyes to their lies, their pride, their oppression, and their injustice. Turn them around, O Lord, so they may repent and follow You, embracing love, kindness, and peace. May they stop their oppression, cruelty, and bloodshed, and may they also come to You, O Jesus Christ, in love and compassion.

Father, save Iran and the Iranian people. Bring freedom to this country and its people. Free us, O Lord, and protect us. Father, in the name of Jesus Christ, send a leader whose heart beats for You and will guide the people toward goodness and joy.

O Father, remove oppression from Iran and establish Your love, grace, and mercy in the land. Reign over Iran, O Lord, as You spoke in Jeremiah 49. O Lord, may Iran become the first Christian country in the Middle East, raising Your light, love, and grace everywhere.

In the name of Jesus Christ,

Amen

## Twenty-Fourth Day
## The Lord Is a refuge for the oppressed

Our devotional today is from Psalm 9, and we continue our prayers for Iran and the Iranian people:

*¹I will praise You, O Lord, with my whole heart; I will tell of all Your marvelous works. ²I will be glad and rejoice in You; I will sing praise to Your name, O Most High. ³When my enemies turn back; they shall fall and perish at Your presence. ⁴For You have maintained my right and my cause. You sat on the throne judging in righteousness. ⁵You have rebuked the nations, You have destroyed the wicked; You have blotted out their name forever and ever. ⁶O enemy, destructions are finished forever! And you have destroyed cities; even their memory has perished. ⁷But the Lord shall endure forever; He has prepared His throne for judgment. ⁸He shall judge the world in righteousness, and He shall administer judgment for the peoples in uprightness. ⁹The Lord also will be a refuge for the oppressed, a refuge in times of trouble. ¹⁰And those who know Your name will put their trust in You; for You, Lord, have not forsaken those who seek You. ¹¹Sing praises to the Lord, who dwells in Zion! Declare His deeds among the people. ¹²When He avenges blood, He remembers them; He does not forget the cry of the humble. ¹³Have mercy on me, O Lord! Consider my trouble from those who hate me, You who lift me up from the gates of death,¹⁴that I may tell of all Your praise. In the gates of the daughter of Zion. I will rejoice in Your salvation. ¹⁵The nations have sunk down in the pit which they made; in the net which they hid, their own foot is caught. ¹⁶The Lord is known by the judgment He executes; The wicked is snared in the work of his own hands. Meditation. Selah.¹⁷The wicked shall be turned into hell and all the nations that forget God.¹⁸For the needy shall not always be forgotten; the expectation of the poor shall not perish forever. [19]Arise, O Lord, do not let man prevail; let the nations be judged in Your sight. [20]Put them in fear, O Lord, that the nations may know themselves to be but men. Selah.*

The Lord, the Lord is the judge, and He is the one who, as His word says, is a fortress for the oppressed; a fortress for the oppressed in times of trouble. O Father, You are the fortress for the oppressed in Iran. You are the one who answers the cries of the people of Iran. You are the one who sees Iran, and You are the one who sees the oppressors.

As Your word says, let fear fall upon them, O Lord. Let fear fall upon them and change their hearts, change their minds. May they also be saved. May they come to know You, O Jesus Christ, and experience Your love, grace, and mercy, O Lord.

O Jesus Christ, You told us to pray for our enemies. We pray for them, O Lord. They need You more than anyone else—those who have taken up arms, those who are oppressing and torturing, they need You most of all. Change their thoughts, change their hearts, and save them.

Save Iran, O Lord. The great work You have started in Iran, we know that You are able to bring it to completion. As Your word says, show them that they are only human and all are under Your power, love, and judgment. Therefore, O Lord, come to the aid of Iran. Set the people of Iran free, free our country from evil, oppression, and injustice, O Lord. Only You are able, O Lord.

And once again, we declare, as Your prophecy in Jeremiah 49 says, that You will establish Your throne over Elam and reign. And You have established it; begin Your reign, O Father. Begin Your reign, O Jesus Christ. Fill our people with Your love, grace, and mercy, and save Iran. May Iran become the first Christian country in the Middle East, spreading Your light, love, and grace to all corners of the world.

In the name of Jesus Christ, Amen

## Twenty-Fifth Day
## The Lord is our helper

Our devotional today is from Psalm 54. We continue to pray for Iran, the situation in Iran, our fellow citizens, and ourselves. The words we read are those that David wrote for the Lord during challenging times:

*¹Save me, O God, by Your name and vindicate me by Your strength. ²Hear my prayer, O God; give ear to the words of my mouth. ³For strangers have risen up against me and oppressors have sought after my life; they have not set God before them. Selah. ⁴Behold, God is my helper; the Lord is with those who uphold my life. ⁵He will repay my enemies for their evil. Cut them off in Your truth. ⁶I will freely sacrifice to You; I will praise Your name, O Lord, for it is good. ⁷For He has delivered me out of all trouble; and my eye has seen its desire upon my enemies.*

Amen

Let us come before the Lord and pray for today.

O Father, we are thankful to You. We praise You, O Lord, for being the refuge for all the oppressed. Your eyes are open, and You see all the suffering, harm, wrongdoings, and goodness, O Lord. Thank You, Father, for being just and for judging righteously. O Father, we bring Iran and our fellow citizens before You. O Lord, grant joy to the broken-hearted. O Lord, comfort those who are grieving.

O Father, You see everything, and nothing is hidden from Your eyes or escapes You, O Lord. You tell us that in times of trouble, You are our refuge. Lord, reveal Yourself to Iran and the Iranian people, to our fellow citizens, Father, so that they may truly know who You are and that Jesus Christ is the only way to You.

Jesus Christ says, *"I am the way and the truth, and no one comes to the Father except through Me."* He says that the path to salvation and righteousness is narrow, but the path that leads to destruction is broad and wide. O Jesus Christ, You are the one who calls, *"Come to Me, the weary and burdened, and I will give you rest. Take My yoke upon you, for My yoke is easy".* And *"I will give you peace—not the peace that the world gives, but My peace I give to you".*

O Jesus Christ, grant Your peace to Iran and the Iranian people. Grant it to us today. Grant upon us our share of joy, happiness, love, grace, patience, and endurance. O Lord, open the eyes. Open the hearts to You, O dear Christ. For You are the Lord of love, compassion, and grace. Place Your hand upon us, O Lord, and save Iran and the Iranian people; set them free, not only physically but spiritually, O Lord, so that those who do not know You may come to know You and experience Your grace, love, compassion, and purity. Open their eyes.

We pray for our enemies; we pray for the wicked. Turn their hearts, O Lord. Have mercy on them. Open their eyes to their wickedness, their mistakes, and their crimes, and turn them around. O Lord, we place Iran in Your hands. Reign over it and make it Your kingdom.

In the name of Jesus Christ,

Amen

# Twenty-Sixth Day
## O Lord, deliver our souls

Today's devotion is from Psalm 116, and it is a prayer for each of us, for Iran, for Iranian people, and for the situation in Iran. Let us read together:

*¹I love the Lord, because He has heard my voice and my supplications.*

Indeed, the Lord has heard the cries of Iran and its people.

*²Because He has inclined His ear to me; therefore I will call upon Him as long as I live. ³The pains of death surrounded me and the pangs of Sheol laid hold of me; I found trouble and sorrow. ⁴Then I called upon the name of the Lord: "O Lord, I implore You, deliver my soul!" ⁵Gracious is the Lord and righteous; yes, our God is merciful. ⁶The Lord preserves the simple; I was brought low and He saved me. ⁷Return to your rest, O my soul, for the Lord has dealt bountifully with you. ⁸For You have delivered my soul from death, my eyes from tears, and my feet from falling.*

You have delivered my soul, and our souls, from death.

*⁹I will walk before the Lord In the land of the living. ¹⁰I believed, therefore I spoke, "I am greatly afflicted." ¹¹I said in my haste, "all men are liars". ¹²What shall I render to the Lord for all His benefits toward me? ¹³I will take up the cup of salvation and call upon the name of the Lord. ¹⁴I will pay my vows to the Lord now in the presence of all His people. ¹⁵Precious in the sight of the Lord is the death of His saints. ¹⁶O Lord, truly I am Your servant; I am Your servant, the son of Your maidservant; You have loosed my bonds. ¹⁷I will offer to You the sacrifice of thanksgiving and will call upon the name of the Lord. ¹⁸I will pay my vows to the Lord now in the presence of all His people, [19]in the courts of the Lord's house, in the midst of you, O Jerusalem.*

Hallelujah, Hallelujah, Hallelujah

I have changed 'I' to 'we' and prayed on behalf of all of us, all Iranians around the world, and all Christians. We bring this prayer, this word, this heartfelt conversation with the Lord before Him and say: You loosen our bonds, the bonds of Iran. With faith, we stand and say: You have loosened the bonds. You have blessed the simple-hearted. You, O Lord, have saved Iran from death and will continue to do so, and You will uplift us and our people.

O Lord, what greater exaltation is there than that all may come and know You, O Jesus Christ, and accept You as Savior, as Lord, and as God? Then we will say, we will call upon the name of the Lord, the name of the Lord. It is written that everyone who calls on the name of the Lord will be saved, and we call on the name of the Lord.

We will pay our vows, offerings, and commitments to You, O Lord. You, O God, have freed Your people, the people of Iran, and You will continue to set them free. You will place Your throne over Iran, and You have already placed it in this very moment, and You will reign.

Bring mercy, kindness, love, health, and grace to Iran, O Lord, just as You have begun this work, bring it to completion. Free Iran, the people of Iran, and Iranians around the world. Lead them to recognize You, O Jesus Christ, as their Lord, and may the Holy Spirit pour peace, tranquility, serenity, intimacy, kindness, and grace upon the people and each of us, bringing salvation.

In the name of Jesus Christ,

Amen

# Twenty-Seventh Day
## The Lord is our refuge and strength

Our devotional for today comes from Psalm 46 and we offer it as a prayer for Iran and our fellow countrymen in Iran:

*[1]God is our refuge and strength, a very present help in trouble. [2]Therefore we will not fear, even though the earth be removed, and though the mountains be carried into the midst of the sea; [3]though its waters roar and be troubled, though the mountains shake with its swelling. Selah. [4]There is a river whose streams shall make glad the city of God, the holy place of the tabernacle of the Most High. [5]God is in the midst of her, she shall not be moved; God shall help her, just at the break of dawn. [6]The nations raged, the kingdoms were moved; He uttered His voice, the earth melted. [7]The Lord of hosts is with us; the God of Jacob is our refuge. Selah. [8]Come, behold the works of the Lord, who has made desolations in the earth. [9]He makes wars cease to the end of the earth; He breaks the bow and cuts the spear in two; He burns the chariot in the fire. [10]Be still and know that I am God; I will be exalted among the nations, I will be exalted in the earth! [11]The Lord of hosts is with us; the God of Jacob is our refuge. Selah.*

Amen

So, O Lord, O Father, You alone are the refuge and strength of Iran, the Iranians, and us. O Lord, You are the one who swiftly rushes to deliver the people and the oppressed in times of trouble. Hurry, O Lord. Hurry to aid the Iranians, to assist those who are under oppression, injustice, and suffering, O Lord. O Father, everything can tremble, mountains may tremble, and the seas may roar in the storm; but when You are present, when You are our refuge, there is no fear. Be the refuge for Iran and the Iranians, O Father. In the place where You are, everything stands firm.

O Lord, Your Word says that You are the one who brings an end to wars. Put an end to the war, strife, injustice, and oppression in Iran as soon as possible, O Father. Your Word says that You are the One who breaks the bow and shatters the spear. Lord, destroy the weapons that have been raised against the people; break them and wipe them out. You are the One who burns the chariots with fire, O Lord.

All the weapons and everything that rises against the people, O Lord, destroy them, and let the people stand and see that You are the Lord, exalted above all nations and over all the earth, for You are the Commander of the Lord's army, O Jesus Christ.

Therefore, O Lord, O Jesus Christ, have mercy on Iran and the Iranian people, and bring salvation to them. Bring salvation to our people and to each of us. Free Iran, end the wars, and let Your name be exalted in Iran.

In the name of Jesus Christ,

Amen

# Twenty-Eighth Day
## Our help comes from the Lord

Our devotional today is from Psalm 121. We continue our prayer for Iran, our fellow countrymen in Iran, and ourselves with these words from the Lord:

*¹I will lift up my eyes to the hills—from whence comes my help? ²My help comes from the Lord, who made heaven and earth. ³He will not allow your foot to be moved. He who keeps you will not slumber. ⁴Behold, He who keeps Israel,*

Yes, He keeps Iran.

*shall neither slumber nor sleep. ⁵The Lord is your keeper; the Lord is your shade at your right hand. ⁶The sun shall not strike you by day, nor the moon by night. ⁷The Lord shall preserve you from all evil; He shall preserve your soul. ⁸The Lord shall preserve your going out and your coming in, from this time forth, and even forevermore.*

Amen

O Father, we come with our eyes fixed only on You. Our eyes remain solely on You, O Jesus Christ, our Lord. You alone are the Creator of heaven and earth and all that is within them. You alone are the refuge and support of us Iranians and of Iran. Our help comes only from You, O Father—only from You.

We trust, O Lord, that You will not allow our feet or the steps of Iran to be shaken. We know that You are our Protector, never sleeping, never closing Your eyes, O Lord.

Yes, Lord, You are the Protector of Iran and its people. Father, as Your word declares, You do not abandon Iran or its people; You remain with them like their shadow, in constant presence. Neither the sun, the moon, nor any form of oppression or injustice will overcome Iran and its people, for You, Father, are righteous, good, merciful, and full of love. And it is You, Lord, who has declared that You will establish Your throne over Iran and its people and that You will reign.

Reign Father. reign over Iran, over our hearts, and over the hearts of our fellow countrymen. O Jesus Christ, reveal Yourself and bring salvation to all Iranians and to the land of Iran.

O Lord, everything we have is in Your hands—our lives, our homeland, and our every step, which You, Father, watch over. We entrust everything to You and believe, O Lord, that You will help, that You will cleanse Iran from oppression and injustice, and that You will establish Your love, kindness, and peace over the nation. Thank You, Father.

In the name of Jesus Christ,

Amen

## Twenty-Ninth Day
## Father, build Iran upon Your Rock

I am currently in Vila Dela, Victoria, Brazil, atop a large rock where one of the first churches was established. Here, in the house of the Lord and one of His churches, I would like us to pray together for Iran, our fellow countrymen, and the issues unfolding in Iran.

Father, we thank You and are grateful for all Your goodness, beauty, and the magnificent places You have created in nature. Father, we bring Iran and the Iranian people before You, O Lord; in the name of Jesus Christ, heal them and deliver them from oppression and injustice. Grant them freedom so that they too may be like Your House, built upon a great rock, built upon Your Rock. Just as You have established this house upon this rock, O Lord, build Iran upon a great rock, Your Rock, Jesus Christ, which will never be shaken. Grant them peace, freedom, and deliverance.

We thank You, Father, for hearing our voice. In the name of Jesus Christ, our Lord, grant freedom, justice, love, and peace to Iran and the Iranian people.

Amen

# Thirtieth Day
## Father, deliver the Iranian people from their enemy

Our devotional today is based on Psalm 59:

*¹Deliver me from my enemies, O my God.*

O Lord, deliver Iran and the Iranian people from their enemies.

*Defend me from those who rise up against me.*

Defend Iran and Iranians from those who rise up against them.

*²Deliver me from the workers of iniquity and save me from bloodthirsty men.*

Lord, deliver us from workers of iniquity and save us from bloodthirsty men.

*³For look, they lie in wait for my life; the mighty gather against me, not for my transgression nor for my sin, O Lord. ⁴They run and prepare themselves through no fault of mine. Awake to help me and behold! ⁵You therefore, O Lord God of hosts, the God of Israel, awake to punish all the nations; do not be merciful to any wicked transgressors. Selah. ⁶At evening they return, they growl like a dog and go all around the city. ⁷Indeed, they belch with their mouth; swords are in their lips; for they say, "Who hears?" ⁸But You, O Lord, shall laugh at them. You shall have all the nations in derision. ⁹I will wait for You, O You his strength; for God is my defense.*

We will wait for You, for You, O God, are our defense.

*¹⁰My God of mercy shall come to meet me; God shall let me see my desire on my enemies.*

Our God of mercy shall come to meet us and shall let us see our desire on our enemies.

*<sup>11</sup>Do not slay them, lest my people forget; scatter them by Your power, and bring them down, O Lord our shield. <sup>12</sup>For the sin of their mouth and the words of their lips, let them even be taken in their pride, and for the cursing and lying which they speak.*

Amen

Father, You have heard our voice for our homeland, Iran—for the Iranian people both within the country and those living abroad who are suffering under oppression and injustice, especially our Christian brothers and sisters. Lord, in the name of Jesus Christ, pour out Your power and be their shield. Transform the hearts of the wicked, Lord, and save them. Turn them back and set Iran and its people free from the grip of evil, for our struggle is not against flesh and blood but against the rulers and forces of darkness in the heavenly realm.

Lord, remove the power, strength, and force that drive them, and save them as well. Lift up Iran and its people under Your mighty hand. We bring before You the oppressed, the broken-hearted, those who have lost loved ones, and those imprisoned, Lord, that You may be their shield and refuge. Strengthen them, lift them up, comfort them, heal their hearts, and restore them, Father.

We pray in the name of Jesus Christ, our Lord, and receive it in faith,

Amen

# Thirty-First Day
## Lord, grant us Your grace

Our devotional today is from Psalm 57:

*¹Be merciful to me, O God, be merciful to me! For my soul trusts in You; and in the shadow of Your wings I will make my refuge, until these calamities have passed by. ²I will cry out to God Most High, to God who performs all things for me. ³He shall send from heaven and save me.*

He shall save us and Iran.

*He reproaches the one who would swallow me up. Selah. God shall send forth His mercy and His truth. ⁴My soul is among lions; I lie among the sons of men who are set on fire, whose teeth are spears and arrows, and their tongue a sharp sword. ⁵Be exalted, O God, above the heavens; let Your glory be above all the earth. ⁶They have prepared a net for my steps; my soul is bowed down; they have dug a pit before me; into the midst of it they themselves have fallen. Selah.*

They set a trap for our feet, and our souls were weighed down. They dug a pit in our path, but they themselves have fallen into it.

*⁷My heart is steadfast, O God, my heart is steadfast; I will sing and give praise. ⁸Awake, my glory! Awake, lute and harp! I will awaken the dawn. ⁹I will praise You, O Lord, among the peoples; I will sing to You among the nations.*

Lord, we will praise You among the nations and sing of You among the nations.

*¹⁰For Your mercy reaches unto the heavens, and Your truth unto the clouds. ¹¹Be exalted, O God, above the heavens; let Your glory be above all the earth.*

Amen

Amen, O Lord. As Your Word says, Lord, You are the refuge of our souls, of all of us, and of Iran and its people. It is under Your wings that we, Iranians and Iran, find shelter, so that You may deliver us from calamity, O Lord. We know, O Lord, and we believe that Your mercy and truth will reach Iran and its people, and You will save them, O Lord. O Lord, the lives of our fellow countrymen in Iran are among lions. They lie among the sons of men who are set on fire, whose teeth are sharp.

O Lord, we trust that You will send help. Arise, O Lord, and save Iran and its people. Grant patience to the grieving and oppressed, and give them joy and comfort, O Lord. May all of us be steadfast in You, in the Lord Jesus Christ, and may we sing to You. May Iran and its people sing for You, O Jesus Christ, for You are powerful, full of mercy and truth, and You will deliver Iran.

In the name of Jesus Christ,

Amen

# Thirty-Second Day
## Your love for us Is great

We continue today's devotion with Psalm 86, offering our prayers for Iran, our fellow countrymen, and ourselves through this psalm.

Wherever the psalm speaks of the individual, we can extend it to include Iran, its people, and ourselves, making it a prayer for our homeland in these times:

*[1]Bow down Your ear, O Lord, hear me; for I am poor and needy. [2]Preserve my life, for I am holy; You are my God; save Your servant who trusts in You! [3]Be merciful to me, O Lord, for I cry to You all day long. [4]Rejoice the soul of Your servant,*

Yes, O Lord, we cry to You all day long. 4Rejoice the soul of Iran and its people, O Lord.

*For to You, O Lord, I lift up my soul. [5]For You, Lord, are good, and ready to forgive, and abundant in mercy to all those who call upon You. [6]Give ear, O Lord, to my prayer and attend to the voice of my supplications. [7]In the day of my trouble I will call upon You, for You will answer me. [8]Among the gods there is none like You, O Lord; nor are there any works like Your works.*

There is none like You, O Father. There is none like You, O Jesus Christ.

*[9]All nations whom You have made shall come and worship before You, O Lord, and shall glorify Your name. [10]For You are great and do wondrous things; You alone are God.*

You alone are God, O Father.

*[11]Teach me Your way, O Lord; I will walk in Your truth; unite my heart to fear Your name. [12]I will praise You, O Lord my God,*

*with all my heart, and I will glorify Your name forevermore. ¹³For great is Your mercy toward me and You have delivered my soul from the depths of Sheol.*

Your mercy is great toward us, O Lord. You have delivered our souls from the depths of Sheol.

*¹⁴O God, the proud have risen against me, and a mob of violent men have sought my life and have not set You before them.*

*¹⁵But You, O Lord, are a God full of compassion, and gracious, Longsuffering and abundant in mercy and truth. ¹⁶Oh, turn to me and have mercy on me! Give Your strength to Your servant and save the son of Your maidservant. ¹⁷Show me a sign for good, that those who hate me may see it and be ashamed, because You, Lord, have helped me and comforted me.*

Amen

Amen. Lord, Father, we bring the people of Iran and the nation of Iran before You, for Your love and mercy extend from the earth to the heavens. You, Lord, are good, generous, and full of love. Hear our prayers and supplications, Father. There is no one like You; You alone are Lord. Father, Son, and Holy Spirit, bring to completion the work You have begun in Iran. End oppression and injustice, Lord. Grant salvation and spiritual deliverance through Jesus Christ to all, and rescue Iran and its people from this persecution.

In the name of Jesus Christ,

Amen

# Thirty-Third Day
## Our Rock and Fortress

Today's devotion is inspired by Psalm 144:

*[1]Blessed be the Lord my Rock, who trains my hands for war and my fingers for battle— [2]my lovingkindness and my fortress, my high tower and my deliverer, my shield and the One in whom I take refuge, who subdues my people under me.*

He is our lovingkindness, our high tower and our deliverer, our shield and the One in whom we take refuge, who subdues our people under us. *[3]Lord, what is man, that You take knowledge of him? Or the son of man, that You are mindful of him? [4]Man is like a breath; his days are like a passing shadow. [5]Bow down Your heavens, O Lord, and come down; touch the mountains and they shall smoke. [6]Flash forth lightning and scatter them; shoot out Your arrows and destroy them. [7]Stretch out Your hand from above; rescue me and deliver me out of great waters, from the hand of foreigners, [8]whose mouth speaks lying words and whose right hand is a right hand of falsehood. [9]I will sing a new song to You, O God; on a harp of ten strings, I will sing praises to You. [10]The One who gives salvation to kings, who delivers David His servant from the deadly sword. [11]Rescue me and deliver me from the hand of foreigners, whose mouth speaks lying words and whose right hand is a right hand of falsehood— [12]that our sons may be as plants grown up in their youth; that our daughters may be as pillars, sculptured in palace style; [13]that our barns may be full, supplying all kinds of produce; that our sheep may bring forth thousands and ten thousands in our fields; [14]that our oxen may be well laden; that there be no breaking in or going out; that there be no outcry in our streets. [15]Happy are the people who are in such a state; happy are the people whose God is the Lord!*

Amen

So come, O Father, come. Be the stronghold and refuge for Iran and its people. Deliver Iran and its people from the deceitful, the oppressors, and the foreigners, O Lord. Pour Your blessings once more upon Iran, its people, and us, O Lord. Heal Your people, O Lord, with Your boundless love, power, and miracles. Reign over Iran, O Father, and bring all to the knowledge that You alone are God—Father, Son, and Holy Spirit.

Touch them, O Father; heal them. Heal the broken-hearted, restore the afflicted bodies, and set the prisoners free. Bring blessing, mercy, and goodness back to Iran and its people. And the greatest gift is You, O Jesus Christ, the Lord of love and compassion.

May they all come to know You and experience Your peace, serenity, love, and mercy.

In the name of Jesus Christ,

Amen

# Thirty-Fourth Day
## With God's help, we will prevail

Today, our devotional is based on Psalm 108:

*¹O God, my heart is steadfast; I will sing and give praise, even with my glory. ²Awake, lute and harp! I will awaken the dawn. ³I will praise You, O Lord, among the peoples, and I will sing praises to You among the nations. ⁴For Your mercy is great above the heavens and Your truth reaches to the clouds. ⁵Be exalted, O God, above the heavens, and Your glory above all the earth; ⁶that Your beloved may be delivered, save with Your right hand, and hear me.*

Yes, Father, You, O Lord, are worthy of our praise and worship, because Your love extends from the earth to the heavens and from east to west. O Lord, when we were Your enemies, You did not withhold Your Son from us. He was sacrificed on the cross for us, for our sins and curses—an eternal sacrifice. He paid the price for all our wrongdoings and curses; and on the third day, He rose from the dead and was declared righteousness for us. This is what is meant by "Save by Your right hand", Your right hand, Jesus Christ.

O Lord, answer our prayers. We know You hear us and that You listen to our voices, O Jesus Christ. We trust that You always desire and bring the best for those who love You and are called by Your name. Therefore, Father, we come united before You and ask for the deliverance of Iran and its people. O Lord, grant their freedom—not only physical freedom, but spiritual freedom, so that all may come to know You, O Jesus Christ, as their Savior and Lord. May they experience Your grace, love, and mercy, and find Your peace and serenity.

So, dear Christ, pour Your peace and serenity upon Iran and its land, and bring salvation, O Lord. End oppression, injustice, and bloodshed, O God, and may Iran and Elam be under Your throne, as You prophesied in Jeremiah 49, that You would place Your throne there and reign over it.

In the name of Jesus Christ,

Amen

## Thirty-Fifth Day
## The Lord will not cast off His people

Our devotional today is from Psalm 94:

*¹O Lord God, to whom vengeance belongs—O God, to whom vengeance belongs, shine forth! ²Rise up, O Judge of the earth; render punishment to the proud. ³Lord, how long will the wicked, how long will the wicked triumph? ⁴They utter speech and speak insolent things; all the workers of iniquity boast in themselves. ⁵They break in pieces Your people, O Lord, and afflict Your heritage. ⁶They slay the widow and the stranger and murder the fatherless. ⁷Yet they say, "The Lord does not see, nor does the God of Jacob understand." ⁸Understand, you senseless among the people; and you fools, when will you be wise? ⁹He who planted the ear, shall He not hear? He who formed the eye, shall He not see? ¹⁰He who instructs the nations, shall He not correct, He who teaches man knowledge? ¹¹The Lord knows the thoughts of man, that they are futile. ¹²Blessed is the man whom You instruct, O Lord, and teach out of Your law, ¹³that You may give him rest from the days of adversity, until the pit is dug for the wicked. ¹⁴For the Lord will not cast off His people, nor will He forsake His inheritance. ¹⁵But judgment will return to righteousness, and all the upright in heart will follow it.*

Amen

Amen O Lord. Yes, Father, yes, Father, You are the Judge of the earth. You, Lord, judge the proud, the wicked, the oppressors, the murderers, and all others. It is You, Lord, who are the helper and supporter of Iran and its people, Your land and heritage, Lord, for Your Word says that a day will come when You, Jesus Christ, will set Your throne upon Iran and reign.

Lord, today that time has come for the prophecy of Jeremiah 49 to be fulfilled, for You, Jesus Christ, to place Your throne upon Iran and remove all wickedness, crime, murder, and bloodshed from this country and its people. For You Lord, You see, and You hear the cries and groans of the oppressed. You hear the voices of widows and orphans, and You Lord, will take vengeance. You Lord, will set everything right; Your judgment is always good and everlasting.

O Father, following You and walking with You, Jesus Christ, brings righteousness, mercy, peace, serenity, and tranquility. Therefore, Father, Jesus Christ, Holy Spirit, pour these upon Iran and mend the broken hearts. Turn laments into laughter, Lord; only You are capable. Grant Your peace and serenity upon all Iranians. Lead them to recognize You as the Lord and Savior, the only path to the Father. Deliver Your land, Iran, and Your people, Lord.

In the name of Jesus Christ,

Amen

# Thirty-Sixth Day
## Who will rise up for Me against the evildoers?

Our devotional continues with Psalm 94, as we extend our prayers for Iran, Iranian people, and ourselves:

*<sup>16</sup>Who will rise up for me against the evildoers? Who will stand up for me against the workers of iniquity? <sup>17</sup>Unless the Lord had been my help; my soul would soon have settled in silence. <sup>18</sup>If I say, "My foot slips," Your mercy, O Lord, will hold me up. <sup>19</sup>In the multitude of my anxieties within me, Your comforts delight my soul. <sup>20</sup>Shall the throne of iniquity, which devises evil by law, have fellowship with You? <sup>21</sup>They gather together against the life of the righteous and condemn innocent blood. <sup>22</sup>But the Lord has been my defense and my God the rock of my refuge. <sup>23</sup>He has brought on them their own iniquity and shall cut them off in their own wickedness; the Lord our God shall cut them off.*

Amen

Amen. Amen. Yes, Lord. Yes, Father. Yes, Jehovah. You are the one who rises against the wicked. Yes, Lord, You stand for Iran and its people against evildoers. Lord, if You were not our helper, everything would have ended by now, and all would have perished. But, Lord, Your love is the refuge for Iran, its people, and us. In the multitude of sorrows in our hearts and the grief of Iran's mourners, You are the comfort and joy of our souls, Father. Jesus Christ, pour Your love, grace, peace, and tranquility upon Iran, its people, and each of us.

O Father, we know that You oppose the wicked and support the righteous. Those who stand against the righteous shed blood and issue death decrees for children and people; O Father, demonic forces empower them. Therefore, Lord, confront these demonic forces that incite people to rise against one another. Turn the pits they have dug against themselves. Save those under the influence of these demons, Lord, so they may come to know You. Let them bow their knees before You, Jesus Christ, and declare that Jesus Christ is Lord. Let them repent of their deeds and receive Your salvation; cease from evil and wickedness, and stand for the people, for love, for justice, and righteousness.

Only You, Father, are capable of saving Iran, the Iranians, and each of us. We pray for Your children, for the Christians who are suffering in Iran, that You may uplift them; they are the salt and light of this world. May we, wherever we are, be Your salt and light, proclaiming and demonstrating Your peace, tranquility, and love to the people. And may You, Jesus Christ, place Your throne upon Elam, Iran, and each of our hearts.

We entrust this day into Your blessed hands, Lord, and declare that You are capable of bringing to completion the work You have begun in the best possible way.

Amen

# Thirty-Seventh Day
## Let us sing to the Lord

Our devotional today is from Psalm 95:

*¹Oh come, let us sing to the Lord! Let us shout joyfully to the Rock of our salvation. ²Let us come before His presence with thanksgiving; let us shout joyfully to Him with psalms. ³For the Lord is the great God and the great King above all gods. ⁴In His hand are the deep places of the earth; the heights of the hills are His also. ⁵The sea is His, for He made it; and His hands formed the dry land. ⁶Oh come, let us worship and bow down; let us kneel before the Lord our Maker. ⁷For He is our God, and we are the people of His pasture, and the sheep of His hand. Today, if you will hear His voice: ⁸"Do not harden your hearts, as in the rebellion, as in the day of trial in the wilderness, ⁹When your fathers tested Me; they tried Me, though they saw My work. ¹⁰For forty years I was grieved with that generation, and said, 'It is a people who go astray in their hearts and they do not know My ways.' ¹¹So I swore in My wrath, 'they shall not enter My rest.'"*

Amen

Amen, O Lord. Today, O Father, we come before You. O Jehovah, we come before You. We sing to You, for You are worthy of praise and worship, O Lord. You are the Creator of the earth, time, seas, mountains, and valleys. O Lord, You alone are God, and there is no one else. You are the Rock of our salvation, and of Iran and the Iranians. O Lord, before You, every knee shall bow. Your Word says that every knee shall bow and every tongue confess that Jesus Christ is Lord.

O Lord, open our ears to hear Your voice, and if we hear Your voice, O Lord, let us respond to You. Let us not close our ears or shut our eyes to the great works You are doing.

O Lord, forty years, forty-four years have passed since the wicked have reigned. You allowed this, O Lord, so that the truth may be revealed and set the people free. This truth is that Jesus Christ is the only way to the Father; the only way to salvation is Jesus Christ, His blood on the cross, and His resurrection on the third day. The only truth is that the Father, the Son, and the Holy Spirit are one, and they love us so much that they did not withhold anything, not even the life of the Son, from us.

You have allowed us to know the truth, and the truth will set Iran, the Iranians, and us free. Thank You, O Father, for You are capable and You reign. And now, O Lord, forty years have passed. Now is the time, O Father, to bring Iran to the Promised Land, to freedom, to love, to grace, and to goodness.

O Father, open the doors of heaven and pour Your blessings and goodness upon the Iranians so that all may hear Your voice, O Jesus Christ, and believe in You and be saved. Not only physical salvation but spiritual salvation. And remove the wicked, the evil ones, and the evil spirit from Iran and the Iranians, and make Iran once again a free country with free people, people who love You, O Jesus Christ. In the name of the Lord, Jesus Christ, we pray and receive by faith,

Amen

# Thirty-Eighth Day
## Our eyes are upon Your hands, O Father

Our devotional today is from Psalm 123:

*¹Unto You I lift up my eyes, O You who dwell in the heavens.*
*²Behold, as the eyes of servants look to the hand of their masters,*
*as the eyes of a maid to the hand of her mistress, so our eyes look*
*to the Lord our God, until He has mercy on us. ³Have mercy on us,*
*O Lord, have mercy on us! For we are exceedingly filled with*
*contempt. ⁴Our soul is exceedingly filled with the scorn of those*
*who are at ease, with the contempt of the proud.*

Amen

O Father, we come before You, we come before You and say,
O Father, O Jesus Christ, our eyes are fixed upon Your loving
hands, Your generous hands, Your hands full of grace and
kindness, O Lord. O Lord, we know and believe that when we
come before You, pray together, and speak with You, You hear
our words and prayers and respond, O Father, because You are a
good Father.

Jesus Christ tells us that if you, being an earthly father, when
your son asks you for bread, would you give him a stone? How
much more will your Father who is in heaven give you good
things?

We know, Father, that You are good, You are excellent, You
are the best, You are just, You are kind, You see everything, and
nothing escapes Your sight.

O Father, today be with each of us, with each believer. Let us,
O Lord, keep our eyes fixed on You, O Jesus Christ. May our focus
today and every day be on You, O Lord, and may we trust that
whatever happens around us, You, O Lord, desire, provide, and

protect the best for Your children. Therefore, today, O Lord, we entrust this day into Your blessed hands.

Father, You see and know the situation of Iran, the Iranians, and our fellow countrymen. Nothing escapes Your sight. You are aware of the deeds of the proud, the wicked, and the spirits behind them, O Lord. Therefore, Father, in the name of Jesus Christ, which is above every name on earth, under the earth, and in heaven, we stand against the demonic powers, evil forces, demons, and devils that are reigning in Iran.

Father, forty years have passed. The time has now come. Have mercy, O Lord, on Iran and the Iranians, and free the land upon which You promised to establish Your throne. Free the people. Grant inner joy to the suffering and oppressed hearts, O Lord. Lift them up and protect them; bring an end to oppression, crime, and bloodshed. You are capable, O Father, of accomplishing all this.

Pour Your Holy Spirit upon Iran and the Iranians, and grant them salvation. And us as well, O Lord, for we know You, O Jesus Christ, and every day we place ourselves in Your hands, saying, O Lord, O Jesus Christ, cleanse us daily with Your blood and guide us with Your Holy Spirit.

We pray in the name of Jesus Christ, our Lord,

Amen

# Thirty-Ninth Day
## Peace and health be upon Iran

Our devotional today is from Psalm 125:

*¹Those who trust in the Lord are like Mount Zion, which cannot be moved, but abides forever. ²As the mountains surround Jerusalem, so the Lord surrounds His people from this time forth and forever. ³For the scepter of wickedness shall not rest on the land allotted to the righteous, lest the righteous reach out their hands to iniquity. ⁴Do good, O Lord, to those who are good, and to those who are upright in their hearts. ⁵As for such as turn aside to their crooked ways, the Lord shall lead them away with the workers of iniquity. Peace be upon Israel!*

Amen

Father, our trust is solely in You, O Lord, our steadfast Rock and mighty mountain that never moves. When we place our trust in You, stand upon You, and lean on You, we too will never be shaken, for You stand firm, unwavering and unshaken, for all eternity. We will stand firm forever, because we rely on You, our Rock and refuge.

O Lord, just as the mountains surround the cities, protecting them from the attacks of enemies, You, O Father, O Jesus Christ, greater than any mountain and more steadfast than any mountain, surround us—those who have chosen You, O Jesus Christ, as our Savior and Lord—and protect us, keeping Your people safe.

O Father, surround the people of Iran and Iran itself, protecting them from evils, transgressions, and oppressions, just as You have protected and continue to protect the righteous and pure-hearted.

We bring the people of Iran before You, O Father; have mercy. Your love for the people of Iran is from the earth to heaven. O

Father, and lead them to recognize You, O Jesus Christ, as Lord, so they may receive Your peace, tranquility, mercy, and grace.

O Lord, You do not allow the land allotted to the righteous to be trampled by the hands of the wicked. You preserve Your people, lest they also turn to crooked ways.

O Lord, O Father, assist the people of Iran; remove oppression from them. O God, cast out the oppressors. Turn their hearts toward You, O Father, and heal their hearts so that they may hate sin and come to the One who alone is capable of removing and cleansing sins: Jesus Christ, the Savior and Son of God. O Jesus Christ, reign over Iran and the Iranians, O Lord; may Your peace be with Iran and the Iranians. Father, complete the work You began in Iran.

We pray for all faithful Iranians, O Lord; protect them. O God, help each of us, wherever we are, to act as Your salt and light, guiding people toward You, O Jesus Christ. Save them, O Lord. In the name of Jesus Christ, we entrust this day into Your blessed hands, knowing that You are able to complete the work You have begun.

Amen

## Fortieth Day
## Our soul waits for the Lord

We continue our devotional journey through the Book of Psalms. Today, we reflect on Psalm 130, lifting it as a prayer on behalf of Iran, its people, and ourselves:

*¹Out of the depths I have cried to You, O Lord; ²Lord, hear my voice! Let Your ears be attentive to the voice of my supplications. ³If You, Lord, should mark iniquities, O Lord, who could stand? ⁴But there is forgiveness with You, that You may be feared. ⁵I wait for the Lord, my soul waits, and in His word I do hope. ⁶My soul waits for the Lord more than those who watch for the morning— yes, more than those who watch for the morning. ⁷O Israel, hope in the Lord; for with the Lord there is mercy, and with Him is abundant redemption. ⁸And He shall redeem Israel from all his iniquities.*

Let us come before the Lord in prayer:

Father, we lift up the people of Iran, who are enduring oppression and suffering. They cry out to You from the depths of their hearts, O Lord. I know, O Lord, that You hear each of our voices. I know, O Lord, that You listen to the cries of our hearts, and Your ears are open to our pleas and supplications. For You, O Lord, are gracious, kind, and just. You are the One who responds to the hearts of the oppressed, the wronged, the orphans, and the widows, O Lord.

O Father, open the doors, O Lord, open the doors, O Father, for all the people of Iran, that they too may come to know Your love, grace, and purity, O Jesus Christ. It is written, *"If You mark our sins, who could stand before You?"* O Jesus Christ, you took on flesh and dwelled among us. You bore the weight of sin and death and overcame it through the cross. When we were still Your enemies, You died for us. You defeated Satan, evil, and death itself, and You rose again to give us life.

So, we ask You now to pour out this victory upon Iran. Let the people of Iran experience the cleansing of sin, the healing of hearts, and the joy of redemption. May Your peace and justice prevail in the land that has long groaned under the burden of cruelty and falsehood. Reign, O Father, in each of us.

Our hope is in Your word, O Lord, our hope is in You. As Your word says, our hope is in You, and our eyes are set on You, more than the watchman waits for the morning. Yes, O Lord, Iran places its hope in You, for love is found only in You, O Father, and You alone hold salvation. Your word says that abundant salvation is with You.

Therefore, O Lord, deliver Iran and its people from this oppression, injustice, and from the hands of the wicked. End these killings and this injustice, O Father. And those who are cruel, oppressive, deceitful, and criminal, O Lord, change their hearts, save them as well, so they may turn from their evil ways and, through this, defeat the true enemy, Satan, whom You have already triumphed over on the cross.

So today, O Lord, we surrender our lives into Your blessed hands. Reign over our lives, reign over each of us. Open our eyes so that we may behold Your beautiful face, O Jesus Christ, and open our ears so that we may hear Your beautiful voice, O Lord. With Your peace, tranquility, and mercy, save each of us and Iran.

In the name of Jesus Christ,

Amen

# Forty-First Day
## We give thanks to the Lord

Our devotional today is from Psalm 138:

*[1] I will praise You with my whole heart; before the gods I will sing praises to You. [2] I will worship toward Your holy temple and praise Your name for Your lovingkindness and Your truth; for You have magnified Your word above all Your name. [3] In the day when I cried out, You answered me and made me bold with strength in my soul. [4] All the kings of the earth shall praise You, O Lord, when they hear the words of Your mouth. [5] Yes, they shall sing of the ways of the Lord, for great is the glory of the Lord. [6] Though the Lord is on high, yet He regards the lowly; but the proud He knows from afar. [7] Though I walk in the midst of trouble, You will revive me; You will stretch out Your hand against the wrath of my enemies, and Your right hand will save me. [8] The Lord will perfect that which concerns me; Your mercy, O Lord, endures forever; do not forsake the works of Your hands.*

Yes, Father, today we come and praise You with all our hearts and souls. We thank You, Father, and we thank You, Jesus Christ, for Your boundless love, for Your name—the name that is above every name in heaven, on earth, and under the earth—and for Your powerful word, which stands above all things. Your word declares, *"Heaven and earth will pass away, but My words will never pass away"*. And Your word will always accomplish what you have purposed.

We thank You, O Lord, that whenever we call upon You, You answer us. You deliver us, O Jesus Christ. We are grateful. And more than anything, O Lord, when we call upon You, You give us courage. O Father, hear the cry of the hearts of the people of Iran and of Iran, and I know You hear it. Deliver them, answer them, and fill their hearts with courage. Remove fear and anxiety, O Lord, and pour out Your love, mercy, and compassion upon them and all of us Iranians, O Lord.

Your word says, *"Every knee will bow, and every tongue will confess that Jesus Christ is Lord."* O Lord, we will witness the day when kings and rulers, upon hearing Your word, will fall to their knees before You, O Jesus Christ, and praise You. So, O Lord, open the ears of our people to Your word. Open their eyes to Your beauty, peace, serenity, and tranquility, for when they were all Your enemies, You went to the cross for them, O Jesus Christ.

O Lord, may they also come, like us, and sing songs in praise of You. We, who know You, come today and sing songs for You, declaring that You alone are worthy of worship, You alone are worthy, O Lamb of God. You alone save, You alone are the way and the truth, You are the light of this world. Shine upon us and upon all Iranians and Iran.

O Lord, rise up against our enemies, remove the wicked one. Father, establish love, grace, peace, and unity in each of us, in Iran, and among Iranians. We surrender this day into Your blessed hands, and our eyes are on Your blessed hands to see how You bring salvation and pour out Your peace, love, and mercy upon us and the people of Iran.

Do Your work, Father, the work You have begun in us, in Iran, and in each Iranian. Father, complete it; perfect it, O Lord, and save and set us free so that we may be free in You. Reign in the hearts of each of us, O Lord. We surrender this day into Your blessed hands, O Jesus Christ. May You increase, and may we decrease.

Amen

# Forty-Second Day
## Father, You are aware of all things

Our devotional today is from Psalm 139:

*¹O Lord, You have searched me and known me. ²You know my sitting down and my rising up; You understand my thoughts afar off. ³You comprehend my path and my lying down, and are acquainted with all my ways. ⁴For there is not a word on my tongue, but behold, O Lord, You know it altogether. ⁵You have hedged me behind and before and laid Your hand upon me. ⁶Such knowledge is too wonderful for me; It is high, I cannot attain it. ⁷Where can I go from Your Spirit? Or where can I flee from Your presence? ⁸If I ascend into heaven, You are there; if I make my bed in hell, behold, You are there. ⁹If I take the wings of the morning and dwell in the uttermost parts of the sea, ¹⁰even there Your hand shall lead me and Your right hand shall hold me. ¹¹If I say, "surely the darkness shall fall on me," even the night shall be light about me; ¹²indeed, the darkness shall not hide from You, but the night shines as the day; the darkness and the light are both alike to You.*

Amen

Let us pray together.

O Lord, yes, Father, You have tested us, all our fellow countrymen, and Iran. You teach us and know us. You are aware of every action of ours, the actions of Iranians and Iran. O Lord, You know our thoughts before we speak, before we make a request, before we utter a word. You know them, Father.

O Lord, You are present everywhere, and You have surrounded us, Iranians, and Iran from all sides. You have placed Your hand upon us and upon Iran, and You continue to do so, O Lord.

May we open our eyes and witness this great and marvelous blessing, O Lord; for although we do not see You, You are always with us, our constant refuge and protector, always watching over us. Wherever we go, You are there, O Lord. Whether in the heavens, in the depths of the earth, or in the farthest seas, You are there. When the night is dark, we may think we have hidden from You, but You are everywhere, for darkness is as light to You.

You are the light of the world, O Jesus Christ; You, O Lord, are the water of life, O Jesus Christ. Shine Your light into the deepest places. Illuminate every hidden place, every shadow. So shine, Lord—shine upon of violence, hatred, and injustice. Deliver the people of Iran from the grip of evil. Save them from crime, corruption, and bloodshed. Save them from the hands of the wicked. Our battle is not against flesh and blood, but against the heavenly forces, evil spirits, demons, and the devil, O Lord. Father, in the name of Jesus Christ, touch the hearts of those who have taken up arms and are destroying the people, and save them, O Lord. We pray for the Iranian army, that they may join the people.

Father, bring a leader whose heart beats for You, and guide the people, Iran, and the Iranians, O Father, freeing them from the wicked. Turn the wicked around so that they too may fall on their knees, worship You, and have their hearts and minds transformed. Save them, O Lord. Be with each of us today, O Lord. Open our eyes to the truth that You are always with us; there is no place where You are not. If we do not feel Your presence, it is because of us, not You. You have promised to be with us in all circumstances, everywhere. You will never leave us. We thank You for Your presence, and we thank You for Your existence. We entrust this day into Your loving, beautiful, and full of love hands. Open our eyes and ears to Your truth and Your beautiful word, and use us for Your mercy and for Your kingdom.

In the name of Jesus Christ, Amen

## Forty-Third Day
## O Lord, how great are Your works!

Our devotional today is from Psalm 92:

*<sup>1</sup>It is good to give thanks to the Lord, and to sing praises to Your name, O Most High; <sup>2</sup>to declare Your lovingkindness in the morning, and Your faithfulness every night, <sup>3</sup>on an instrument of ten strings, on the lute, and on the harp, with harmonious sound. <sup>4</sup>For You, Lord, have made me glad through Your work; I will triumph in the works of Your hands. <sup>5</sup>O Lord, how great are Your works! Your thoughts are very deep. <sup>6</sup>A senseless man does not know, nor does a fool understand this. <sup>7</sup>When the wicked spring up like grass and when all the workers of iniquity flourish, it is that they may be destroyed forever. <sup>8</sup>But You, Lord, are on high forevermore. <sup>9</sup>For behold, Your enemies, O Lord, for behold, Your enemies shall perish; all the workers of iniquity shall be scattered. <sup>10</sup>But my horn You have exalted like a wild ox; I have been anointed with fresh oil. <sup>11</sup>My eye also has seen my desire on my enemies; my ears hear my desire on the wicked who rise up against me. <sup>12</sup>The righteous shall flourish like a palm tree, he shall grow like a cedar in Lebanon. <sup>13</sup>Those who are planted in the house of the Lord shall flourish in the courts of our God. <sup>14</sup>They shall still bear fruit in old age; they shall be fresh and flourishing, <sup>15</sup>To declare that the Lord is upright; He is my rock, and there is no unrighteousness in Him.*

Amen. Amen

So today, we come before You, O Father, and sing praises to Your name, O Jesus Christ. We exalt You. This morning, we come into Your presence, and before we sleep at night, we declare Your mighty works because You, O Father, are great. You are full of love, power, and faithfulness. You alone, O Lord, whose thoughts are profound.

O Lord, the wicked, the ruthless, the ignorant, and all those who oppress Iran, its people, and others do not understand this. May You open their eyes so they, too, may see Your mighty works, Your boundless love, and Your great grace, O Jesus Christ, and turn away from their evil ways.

And we trust, Lord, that just as Your Word says, You will increase our strength. You will raise up the people of Iran, anoint them with fresh oil, and consecrate them for Yourself.

We are grateful, O Lord. We are confident in this: our ears will hear, and our eyes will see the downfall of wickedness. We will witness Iran's deliverance with our own eyes, and we will hear the shouts of freedom and joy in our own ears—because You, O Lord, are faithful. There is no trace of injustice in You, O Father. No shadow of unfairness exists in You, O Jesus Christ.

Those who are in You, who have accepted You as Lord, Savior, and Protector, and who stand firm in You—just as You are unshaken, so shall we be. For we stand upon our great and steadfast Rock, Jesus Christ. We trust that You are faithful and that You will bring to completion the work You have begun in Iran and in each of us.

Let Your salvation come upon Iran and its people. Let Your salvation be poured out today upon the believers, Your sons and daughters, O Father. May each of us, every night, every day, and every morning, lift up Your name and sing praises to You.

In the name of Jesus Christ,

Amen

## Forty-Fourth Day
## Father, hurry to save us

Our devotional today is from Psalm 141:

*¹Lord, I cry out to You; make haste to me! Give ear to my voice when I cry out to You. ²Let my prayer be set before You as incense, the lifting up of my hands as the evening sacrifice. ³Set a guard, O Lord, over my mouth; keep watch over the door of my lips. ⁴Do not incline my heart to any evil thing, to practice wicked works with men who work iniquity; and do not let me eat of their delicacies. ⁵Let the righteous strike me; it shall be a kindness. And let him rebuke me; it shall be as excellent oil; let my head not refuse it. For still my prayer is against the deeds of the wicked. ⁶Their judges are overthrown by the sides of the cliff, and they hear my words, for they are sweet. ⁷Our bones are scattered at the mouth of the grave, as when one plows and breaks up the earth. ⁸But my eyes are upon You, O God the Lord; in You I take refuge; do not leave my soul destitute. ⁹Keep me from the snares they have laid for me, and from the traps of the workers of iniquity. ¹⁰Let the wicked fall into their own nets, while I escape safely.*

Amen

O Father, we have gathered together as intercessors for Iran and its people—those in Iran who are oppressed and suffering, as well as the rest of the Iranians and believers around the world enduring hardship. Father, You hear our voice. We call upon You, O Father; we call upon You, O Jesus Christ. Hurry to our aid, O Lord. Listen to our cry, and we know You hear us. May our prayers rise like fragrant incense before You, O Lord, and may our hands, lifted in sacrifice, be directed toward You.

O Lord, reign over us—over our tongues, our speech, and our actions, O God. Close, lock, and remove anything that does not belong to You. Increase in us all that is Yours—righteousness, love, and goodness, O Father.

O Father, neutralize the works of the wicked and unjust against us, against Iran, and against the Iranian people. Let the traps they have set for us, for the people, for the believers, for Iran, and for the Iranians, fall upon them instead. And, Father, when they fall into them, may they recognize the truth, O God, and may they come to repentance and turn to You, O Father, O Jesus Christ, and embrace You.

O Father, the crimes, bloodshed, and injustices afflicting Iran and the Iranian people are overwhelming in these times. Yet nothing is hidden from You; You see all things. We come before You, O Lord, and take refuge in You, O God. Therefore, do not leave Iran and its people defenseless, O Father. Deliver us, O God, from these traps, from this oppression and these crimes, and bring us safely through.

We present to You the broken hearts of fathers and mothers, O God. Grant them patience, Your inner peace, and lift them up, O Lord. O Father, bring freedom to Iran and its people, and reign over Iran, its people, and in each of us, O Jesus Christ. Today, pour out Your peace, love, and tranquility upon each of us, upon Iran, and upon the Iranian people, and bring to completion the work You have begun in Iran and in each of us.

In the name of Jesus Christ,

Amen

# Forty-Five Day
## You are our refuge

Our devotional today is from Psalm 142:

*¹I cry out to the Lord with my voice; with my voice to the Lord I make my supplication. ²I pour out my complaint before Him; I declare before Him my trouble. ³When my spirit was overwhelmed within me, then You knew my path. In the way in which I walk, they have secretly set a snare for me. ⁴Look on my right hand and see, for there is no one who acknowledges me; refuge has failed me; no one cares for my soul. ⁵I cried out to You, O Lord: I said, "You are my refuge, my portion in the land of the living. ⁶Attend to my cry, for I am brought very low; deliver me from my persecutors, for they are stronger than I. ⁷Bring my soul out of prison, that I may praise Your name; the righteous shall surround me, for You shall deal bountifully with me."*

Amen. Amen. Let us come together and pray in accordance with this beautiful psalm. O Lord, in these days of persecution and oppression, hear the cries of Iran and its people as they call upon You, O Father, and plead before You, O Lord. They bring their grievances before You and lay their distress at Your feet, O Father. O Lord, look and see—each of their spirits is overwhelmed. See, O God, how the oppressors have blocked their paths and surrounded them, making them feel as though there is no refuge left.

But Father, You—You, O Lord—are our refuge, the refuge of the Iranian people and all who are oppressed. You, O Lord, hear our cries—the cries of all believers and those suffering under oppression and persecution. You, O Lord, know that without You, we are helpless, and if You do not reveal Yourself, we will all perish. O Lord, deliver Iran, its people, and the believers from the hands of the oppressors and those who cause them harm, O Father.

O Father, O Lord, although they are stronger, You are mightier and more terrifying than all. When Your hand is with us, who can stand against us? Your Word says that no weapon formed against You (against us) can stand, for You, O Father, are with us. You are with us; You are with Iran.

We praise Your name and declare that You are the refuge of Iran and the Iranian people, O Father. And we know that in the end, the righteous will be united, and You will show Your mercy to us, to Iran, and to the Iranian people.

Freedom, love, grace, and healing, O Lord, all belong to You, and You, O Jesus Christ, are able to pour them out upon Iran and the Iranian people, bringing them salvation. O Father, send a leader whose heart seeks after Your heart for this nation, O Lord, and set Iran and its people free. Reign over the hearts, spirits, and bodies of the Iranian people and over Iran, O Jesus Christ.

In the name of Jesus Christ,

Amen

# Forty-Sixth Day
## The Lord is great and mighty

Our devotional today comes from Psalm 145:

*[8]The Lord is gracious and full of compassion, slow to anger and great in mercy. [9]The Lord is good to all, and His tender mercies are over all His works. [10]All Your works shall praise You, O Lord, and Your saints shall bless You. [11]They shall speak of the glory of Your kingdom and talk of Your power, [12]to make known to the sons of men His mighty acts and the glorious majesty of His kingdom. [13]Your kingdom is an everlasting kingdom and Your dominion endures throughout all generations. [14]The Lord upholds all who fall and raises up all who are bowed down. [15]The eyes of all look expectantly to You, and You give them their food in due season. [16]You open Your hand and satisfy the desire of every living thing. [17]The Lord is righteous in all His ways, gracious in all His works. [18]The Lord is near to all who call upon Him, to all who call upon Him in truth. [19]He will fulfill the desire of those who fear Him; He also will hear their cry and save them. [20]The Lord preserves all who love Him, but all the wicked He will destroy. [21]My mouth shall speak the praise of the Lord and all flesh shall bless His holy name forever and ever.*

Let us pray, dear ones:

Yes, O Father, You are gracious and merciful. You are slow to anger and abounding in love. You are the One who does good to all, O Lord. Yes, O Father, the works of Your hands— all the works of Your hands— are praised by all of creation, O Lord.

O Lord, reveal Your glory to the people of Iran. Show Your mighty deeds to the people of Iran and to each believer. O Father, Iran is suffering; people are being killed, there is bloodshed, O Lord. Oppression and persecution abound, O Father.

O Lord, You are the faithful God, faithful to Your promises, O Father. You declared that You will deliver Elam. You said that You will establish Your throne over Iran, You will reign, and You will restore and save the people in every way, O Father. Father, You are full of love, full of goodness, O Father. You lift up those who are falling, You take their hand and raise them up. O Lord, take the hands of the fallen in Iran, O Father, and lift them up.

You are the Lord who hears cries and answers. O Father, listen to the cries of the hearts of the Iranians and to all that is happening in Iran, in the Garden of Iran, and in other parts of the country. O Lord, hear, raise Your hand, and deliver, O God.

O Lord, the people are hungry, both physically and spiritually. They are thirsty. Oh Lord, provide for them. Save them, O Lord. Save them, O Lord. God, You have promised to protect all those who love You, so keep them safe, Father. Bring each of them to know You, O Jesus Christ, and let them experience Your love, peace, and comfort.

Lord, we praise You, Father. We praise You, Jesus Christ. For we know that You are our only hope, and You are the hope we have when all seems hopeless. You, O Lord, where there is death, oppression, and injustice, are the hope for life, love, goodness, and salvation.

Father, lift Your hands, save Iran and its people, and protect them. Lord, bring the wicked to their knees so that they too may come to know You and change their ways. Save, O Lord, heal, O Father, and set us free—free each of us, Iran, and the Iranian people.

In the name of Jesus Christ,

Amen

# Forty-Seventh Day
## We place Our trust in the Lord

Our devotional today is from Psalm 146:

*¹Praise the Lord! Praise the Lord, O my soul! ²While I live I will praise the Lord; I will sing praises to my God while I have my being. ³Do not put your trust in princes, nor in a son of man, in whom there is no help. ⁴His spirit departs, he returns to his earth; in that very day his plans perish. ⁵Happy is he who has the God of Jacob for his help, whose hope is in the Lord his God, ⁶Who made heaven and earth, the sea, and all that is in them, Who keeps truth forever, ⁷Who executes justice for the oppressed, Who gives food to the hungry.*

*The Lord gives freedom to the prisoners. ⁸The Lord opens the eyes of the blind; the Lord raises those who are bowed down; the Lord loves the righteous. ⁹The Lord watches over the strangers. He relieves the fatherless and widow; but the way of the wicked He turns upside down. ¹⁰The Lord shall reign forever— Your God, O Zion, to all generations.*

Hallelujah! Hallelujah. Hallelujah

Let us pray together, dear ones. Yes, O Lord, we praise You with all our hearts and with all our being. We sing to You, O Father, with every part of our soul. O Lord, help us not to place our trust in people, in rulers, or in authorities, because they are here today and gone tomorrow. But, O Lord, O Jesus Christ, our hope, our eyes are fixed on You, and only on You, O Lord. We place our full trust in You, O Lord. The hope of Iran, the Iranian people, and all the faithful is found only in You, O Father. For You, O Father, are the One who created the heavens, the earth, the seas, and everything in them.

You are our Creator, full of love, and Lord Jesus Christ, when You were on this earth, You fulfilled all the actions described in this Psalm. You freed the prisoners, delivering those bound by Satan and death with Your own blood. Lord, time and again, Jesus Christ, You restored sight to the blind. You lifted up the fallen, loved the righteous, and showed compassion to strangers (such as the Roman soldier and his servant, and the Roman soldier and his son). You are the protector of orphans and widows; Lord, it was You, Jesus Christ, who raised the son of the widow from death.

But You frustrate the plans of the wicked. We know, Lord, that the paths of the wicked in Iran will come to nothing because You, Lord, are the righteous and compassionate God, and Your kingdom is everlasting. Therefore, our hope, our eyes, and the hope of the Iranian people are fixed on Your beautiful and loving hands, Lord, to free the prisoners, feed the hungry, care for the widows and orphans, and rescue them from the hands of the wicked.

Remove the violence, injustice, and evil from Iran, and establish Your throne of love, grace, peace, and tranquility over Iran. So, Lord, come and fulfill Your work, and save Iran and its people.

In the name of Jesus Christ,

Amen

# Forty-Eighth Day
## The Lord heals the broken-hearted

Our devotional today is from Psalm 147:

*¹Praise the Lord! For it is good to sing praises to our God; for it is pleasant, and praise is beautiful. ²The Lord builds up Jerusalem; He gathers together the outcasts of Israel. ³He heals the broken-hearted and binds up their wounds. ⁴He counts the number of the stars; He calls them all by name. ⁵Great is our Lord, and mighty in power; His understanding is infinite. ⁶The Lord lifts up the humble; He casts the wicked down to the ground. ⁷Sing to the Lord with thanksgiving; sing praises on the harp to our God, ⁸Who covers the heavens with clouds, Who prepares rain for the earth, Who makes grass to grow on the mountains. ⁹He gives to the beast its food, and to the young ravens that cry.*

Amen

Father, You are the Lord, full of love. You hold everything in Your hands. You created all things and know all by name. You alone, Lord, are worthy of our worship and praise.

Lord, You alone have the power to build up Iran. You can bring back those who have been cast out. You can protect Iran, its people, each of us, and every believer. Only You, Jesus Christ, can heal the broken-hearted. Only You can heal the wounded hearts of Iranians, the hearts of our people, and the hearts of those who are here. You alone, Father, have the power—no one else can do this or bind up their wounds. You alone, Lord. We trust in You alone and seek help only from You.

Father, You know all things, and Your understanding is infinite. You are powerful and mighty, full of love. Lord, You embrace the humble and bring down the wicked. Put an end to evil, oppression, persecution, and bloodshed in Iran. Father, come to the aid of the people. Save them, Lord.

Raise up a leader who will guide Your people wholeheartedly for You, Lord. Bring freedom and salvation to Iran, Lord. Rescue our people in Iran, Father. Lord, establish Your throne over Iran and reign with grace, love, purity, and peace.

How long, Lord? How long? You have made a promise. Fulfill it, Lord. Complete the good work. You have begun in Iran and among its people. Drive out evil, silence the wicked, and let Your Spirit reign over the land.

Lord Jesus Christ, we place this day in Your hands—hands full of love and grace. Pour out peace, serenity, and holiness on each of us and on every Iranian. We lift up to You all Your children, especially those in hardship, including the members of our Church. May Your healing and blessing hand be upon them today. Heal, restore, and strengthen their faith. Bless them abundantly.

We pray in the name of Jesus Christ and receive with faith,

Amen

# Forty-Ninth Day
## Hide us from the secret plots of the enemy

Our devotional today is from Psalm 64:

*[1]Hear my voice, O God, in my meditation; preserve my life from fear of the enemy. [2]Hide me from the secret plots of the wicked, from the rebellion of the workers of iniquity, [3]who sharpen their tongue like a sword and bend their bows to shoot their arrows— bitter words, [4]that they may shoot in secret at the blameless; suddenly they shoot at him and do not fear. [5]They encourage themselves in an evil matter; they talk of laying snares secretly; they say, "who will see them?" [6]They devise iniquities: "we have perfected a shrewd scheme." Both the inward thought and the heart of man are deep. [7]But God shall shoot at them with an arrow; suddenly they shall be wounded. [8]So He will make them stumble over their own tongue; all who see them shall flee away. [9]All men shall fear and shall declare the work of God; for they shall wisely consider His doing. [10]The righteous shall be glad in the Lord and trust in Him. And all the upright in heart shall glory.*

Amen

Amen, Lord. Our gracious God and loving Father, we know that when we cry out—when the oppressed, the people of Iran, lift their voices before You—when our lives and theirs are threatened by the enemy, You hear us, Lord. Father, we seek refuge in You alone from the secret plots of the enemy. You alone are our mighty Rock, the only place where we can find shelter and security under the shadow of Your wings. O Lord, hear the cries of the oppressed hearts of the Iranian people and of us as well.

These wicked enemies influenced by the great deceiver Satan, open their mouth, prepare their weapons, and attack the righteous, the innocent, and the defenseless. But Lord, nothing is hidden from

You. They believe their actions go unseen or even justify them as serving You. Open their eyes to see the truth, to recognize how they have fallen under the influence of evil. Lord, transform their hearts, awaken them to reality, and lead them to lay down their weapons and deception. May they repent, turn to You, and stand in defense of the people and the nation.

Father, how long, O Father, will this oppression, injustice, wickedness, and cruelty continue? Arise, O Lord, You are awake, arise, O Lord. O just and merciful Lord, come to the aid of the oppressed and of Iran.

Come to the aid of the grieving, the mothers and fathers who have lost their children, and their brothers and sisters. Let the traps of the wicked fall back upon them. May their arrows be ineffective, may they fall and be overthrown, O God. Bring down the works of the wicked.

Save these people, O Lord. Rise up, O Jesus Christ, and pour out love, compassion, peace, and comfort upon Iran and the people of Iran. Bring freedom to our country, O Lord, and set our fellow citizens free, O God. Our only hope is in You, O Father. No one else can make a difference. So, O Lord, bring to completion the work You have started in Iran, end the oppression and wickedness, put an end to the violence and bloodshed, O Father, and bring everyone to know You, O Jesus Christ, and reign over Iran.

Amen

# The Fiftieth Day
## The Lord is our mighty fortress

Our devotional today is from Psalm 46. In these challenging times for our homeland, Iran, and its people, we lift this Psalm as our prayer to the Lord:

*¹God is our refuge and strength, a very present help in trouble. ²Therefore we will not fear, even though the earth be removed and though the mountains be carried into the midst of the sea; ³though its waters roar and be troubled, though the mountains shake with its swelling. Selah. ⁴There is a river whose streams shall make glad the city of God, the holy place of the tabernacle of the Most High. ⁵God is in the midst of her, she shall not be moved; God shall help her, just at the break of dawn. ⁶The nations raged, the kingdoms were moved; He uttered His voice, the earth melted. ⁷The Lord of hosts is with us; the God of Jacob is our refuge. Selah. ⁸Come, behold the works of the Lord, who has made desolations in the earth. ⁹He makes wars cease to the end of the earth; He breaks the bow and cuts the spear in two; He burns the chariot in the fire. ¹⁰Be still and know that I am God; I will be exalted among the nations, I will be exalted in the earth! ¹¹The Lord of hosts is with us; the God of Jacob is our refuge. Selah.*

O Lord, today we bring our country before You. We bring Iran before You, O Father. You know all things, O Father. You are the Lord, You, O Lord, are the Commander of the heavenly armies, O Jesus Christ. You are the Commander of the Lord's army, O Jesus Christ. Lord, send Your army of angels to Iran. Just as Elijah asks the Lord to open the eyes of his servant so that he may see that the Lord is on our side. When his eyes were opened, he saw that the mountains and fields were filled with Your fiery army of angels. O Lord, send Your army to Iran. O Father, remove the wicked from Iran. Turn the hearts of the oppressors back to You.

Lord, purify and cleanse Iran with Your Holy Spirit. Bring comfort to the suffering and grieving people, O Father. O Jesus Christ, heal their hearts. Open the heavens and respond to this injustice and bloodshed, bringing it to an end. Deliver the people of Iran from their pain and suffering, O Lord. Father, raise up a leader whose heart beats for You, one who can guide the people.

Lord, grant freedom to Iran and the Iranian people, O Father. You are our mighty fortress, O Lord. You are the One who brings an end to all wars through Your Word's name. Bring an end to the war in Iran, O Father. Extend Your loving hand, O Lord, so that all may see and witness Your great works, O Father. You are the One who breaks weapons, bows, and chariots, O Lord. Fulfill Your purpose.

You are the refuge and stronghold of the faithful, of Iran, and of the Iranian people. We seek refuge in You, O Lord. Keep Iran and its people safe in Your fortress, and deliver them from death, oppression, and injustice.

In the name of Jesus Christ,

Amen

# The Fifty-First Day
## My voice You shall hear in the morning, O Lord

Our devotional today is from Psalm 5:

*¹Give ear to my words, O Lord, consider my meditation. ²Give heed to the voice of my cry, my King and my God, for to You I will pray. ³My voice You shall hear in the morning, O Lord; in the morning I will direct it to You and I will look up. ⁴For You are not a God who takes pleasure in wickedness, nor shall evil dwell with You. ⁵The boastful shall not stand in Your sight; You hate all workers of iniquity. ⁶You shall destroy those who speak falsehood; the Lord abhors the bloodthirsty and deceitful man. ⁷But as for me, I will come into Your house in the multitude of Your mercy; in fear of You I will worship toward Your holy temple. ⁸Lead me, O Lord, in Your righteousness because of my enemies; make Your way straight before my face. ⁹For there is no faithfulness in their mouth; their inward part is destruction; their throat is an open tomb; they flatter with their tongue. ¹⁰Pronounce them guilty, O God! Let them fall by their own counsels; cast them out in the multitude of their transgressions, for they have rebelled against You. ¹¹But let all those rejoice who put their trust in You; let them ever shout for joy, because You defend them; let those also who love Your name be joyful in You. ¹²For You, O Lord, will bless the righteous; with favor You will surround him as with a shield.*

Amen

So, dear ones, let us come before the Lord, praying for today, our homeland, Iran, and the Iranian people, bringing them before the feet of the Lord Jesus Christ. Yes, Lord, yes, Jesus Christ, we lift our voices and our words, crying out to You day and night. Iran and its people call upon You, Lord. We turn to You in prayer,

Father. In the midst of these hardships, storms, and darkness, surrounded by oppression, we seek You, Lord.

You are not a God who delights in wickedness. Father, You take no pleasure in evil, and wrongdoing has no place before You. You despise all evildoers and liars. Lord, have mercy on the deceitful and those who shed blood. Open their eyes to see the truth. Turn them back so they may not perish but come to know You, Jesus Christ. May they lay down their weapons, abandon their lies and deceit, and be transformed for good—their own and that of others. You have the power to accomplish all these things, Lord.

We, Your children, come before You and cry out: Lord, have mercy. Have mercy on Iran and its people. Have mercy on those suffering under oppression and injustice. Their suffering is not merely at the hands of others but the work of the evil one. It is the adversary, Satan, who manipulates people to destroy and take the lives of the defenseless.

Jesus Christ, by Your mighty name, drive out the evil one from Iran and restore freedom, love, peace, and stability to the nation. Set Iran and its people free, Lord, so they may worship You freely and wholeheartedly. Lord, Your Word tells us that in the end, those who take refuge in You will be saved. We take refuge in You. As intercessors for Iran and even for those who do not yet know You, we, Your children, stand in the gap and cry out: Lord, save them as well, so they too may ultimately experience Your joy, love, peace, and wholeness. Jesus Christ, bring salvation.

We entrust this day into Your blessed hands. We present Your believers and children before You: Lord, protect them under Your care and shield each of us. Guard our thoughts and hearts from the evil one. Father, help us stand for You wherever we may be. Today and always, strengthen our passion, love, devotion, and faith in You. May Your work, Lord, be fulfilled in each of us, and may the work You have started in Iran come to completion.

We pray in the name of Jesus Christ, our Lord, and receive it in faith, Amen

# The Fifty-Second Day
## In times of hardship, let us praise the Lord and Satan will flee

In recent months, I have been seeking the Lord's guidance about inner joy. The Lord says in His Word: "*the joy of your salvation is your strength*". I asked the Lord, "How can I consistently experience this joy within me?" I have several Christian books on joy, and I have read them.

In one of the books written by Kay Warren, the wife of Rick Warren, author of *The Purpose Driven Life*, she writes: "Joy is knowing that God is aware of every detail of our lives and that everything will work out for our good. Joy is choosing to praise God in every moment and in every circumstance.

Later, one of our Korean friends came and shared a message for both me and Insook. They had also faced many challenges in life, both at home and in different situations. What God had revealed to them, they shared with us: in every circumstance, we should praise, worship, and give thanks to God. They explained that when those around them were causing them distress and anger, God would guide them to begin offering thanks and praise in that moment. They have written several books on worship and praise. In fact, the efforts of the enemy to bring them down, steal their joy, separate them from God, and question His authority, all vanished. Gradually, everything began to work together for their good.

Interestingly, when Peter and Paul were thrown into the darkest dungeon after being flogged, they sang songs of praise to God from the depths of their hearts. Then, an earthquake struck, and the prison doors were opened. When the jailer saw this, he was about to take his own life, but Paul reassured him, saying not to worry, as they were all still there. As a result, the jailer and his entire family were saved, and the name of the Lord was glorified.

Yesterday, as I was praying once again, the Lord revealed to me that "this joy is truly the complete assurance and trust that He is within us, living in us". Always, in every moment, He lives within those of us who have accepted Him as our Lord. This is an inner joy. He reminds us to remember that the One who loves us—the One who loves our soul and gave His life for us— the Creator of this galaxy, the earth, and the heavens; the One who is our Great Shepherd, our greatest Friend, whose love is everlasting, lives within us. He is always with us and will never leave us alone. In truth, this is the joy of our salvation—that He is always with us and we have the Lord living within us.

And what greater joy could there be than this?

When we face storms, things we despise, actions taken against us, and things that rise up against us, when we begin to praise the Lord, and in that moment, we give thanks to God, saying, 'Lord, I thank You even for this—for this storm, for this evil, and for this insult,' we are essentially neutralizing the work that Satan seeks to carry out through these evils and insults—separating us from the Lord and turning our joy into hatred. And when Satan sees that we are doing the exact opposite of his will, he gathers his things and departs.

Today, let us raise the name of the Lord for all the storms, injustices, and challenges taking place in Iran and in our families. In the moments we are attacked, let us lift up the name of the Lord and say, 'Father, thank You. We are grateful. Praise, worship, and adoration for this moment belong to You. I thank You for this storm and for this hardship. I praise You, and in this moment, I lift up Your name because You know all things, You are aware of everything, and You will bring everything to a good end for us. I choose to praise and worship You in every moment.'

Lord, we thank You for what is happening in Iran. We are grateful, O Lord. We praise and worship You in all circumstances. In the midst of this storm, we lift Your name on high and declare that You are the blessed Lord, the Most High, and full of love. We worship You, knowing that You will transform everything for good, in the name of Jesus Christ.

Today, in every moment when you are under attack or faced with things that cause you distress, lift up the name of the Lord and begin to praise Him. Say, 'Thank You, Jesus Christ. Praise be to You, Jesus Christ. Worship and adoration belong to You,

Amen

# The Fifty-Third Day
## Let us praise the Lord, for He Is good

Beloved, our devotional today is based on Psalm 135. Let us come before the Lord in praise and worship, lifting up His holy name:

*¹Praise the Lord! Praise the name of the Lord; praise Him, O you servants of the Lord! ²You who stand in the house of the Lord, in the courts of the house of our God. ³Praise the Lord, for the Lord is good; sing praises to His name, for it is pleasant. ⁴For the Lord has chosen Jacob for Himself, Israel for His special treasure. ⁵For I know that the Lord is great and our Lord is above all gods. ⁶Whatever the Lord pleases He does, in heaven and in earth, in the seas and in all deep places. ⁷He causes the vapors to ascend from the ends of the earth; He makes lightning for the rain; He brings the wind out of His treasuries. ⁸He destroyed the firstborn of Egypt, both of man and beast. ⁹He sent signs and wonders into the midst of you, O Egypt, upon Pharaoh and all his servants. ¹⁰He defeated many nations and slew mighty kings—¹¹Sihon king of the Amorites, Og king of Bashan, and all the kingdoms of Canaan— ¹²and gave their land as a heritage, a heritage to Israel His people. ¹³Your name, O Lord, endures forever, Your fame, O Lord, throughout all generations. ¹⁴For the Lord will judge His people and He will have compassion on His servants. ¹⁵The idols of the nations are silver and gold, the work of men's hands. ¹⁶They have mouths, but they do not speak; eyes they have, but they do not see; ¹⁷They have ears, but they do not hear; nor is there any breath in their mouths. ¹⁸Those who make them are like them; so is everyone who trusts in them. ¹⁹Bless the Lord, O house of Israel! Bless the Lord, O house of Aaron! ²⁰Bless the Lord, O house of Levi! ²¹You who fear the Lord, bless the Lord! ²¹Blessed be the Lord out of Zion, who dwells in Jerusalem!*

Hallelujah! Hallelujah!

Thank You, Lord. All praise belongs to You, Father. You are the Almighty God, and we come before You in every moment and in all circumstances. We give You thanks and praise, knowing that the future is in Your hands and that You want what is best for each of us who know You.

Lord, as intercessors and as Your children, we come before You and say, Lord, grant justice. Lord, help our people in Iran. Lord, assist the Iranians, lift up the oppressed. Lord, do not let them fall to the ground and perish. Cut off the hands of the oppressors, O Lord. Turn the oppressors back so that they may come to know You, fall to their knees, and worship You, Father.

Dear Lord Jesus Christ, today, may Your peace and love be poured out abundantly on each of us who worship You. As we lift Your name at the start of this day, rise within us more and more. Reveal Yourself more and more, and let Your light shine in the darkness of our hearts, our lives, and in the darkness that surrounds Iran. Shine Your light upon Iran, O Lord, O Jesus Christ, and remove the darkness and oppression. Erase the injustices, O Lord, O precious Jesus Christ.

Lord, deliver each of us from the darkness within and from every curse. You carried all of it to the cross. Today, we come before You and ask You to wash our hands and feet each day. You have already cleansed our hearts and souls by Your blood, but in this world, our hands and feet are often stained. Cleanse them again, Lord, so we may walk closely with You and proclaim Your name wherever we go.

Lord, we give thanks for everything happening in Iran. We praise You in our fellow countrymen, in our lives, and in the storms we face. And we say, Lord, we thank You for all of this because we know that, in the end, we will safely reach the shore. Lord, we trust that You will free Iran and its people, and You will reign over our land and the hearts of every one of us Iranians.

Lord, we place this day in Your hands, for You are good, You are the best, You are the greatest, and there is no one better than You,

In the name of Jesus Christ,

Amen

## Fifty-Fourth Day
## Let us give thanks to the Lord,
## for His love endures forever

Our devotional today comes from Psalm 136:

*[1]Oh, give thanks to the Lord, for He is good! For His mercy endures forever. [2]Oh, give thanks to the God of gods! For His mercy endures forever. [3]Oh, give thanks to the Lord of lords! For His mercy endures forever: [4]to Him who alone does great wonders, for His mercy endures forever; [5]to Him who by wisdom made the heavens, for His mercy endures forever; [6]to Him who laid out the earth above the waters, for His mercy endures forever; [7]to Him who made great lights, for His mercy endures forever— [8]the sun to rule by day, for His mercy endures forever; [9]the moon and stars to rule by night, for His mercy endures forever.*

And it goes on to say:

*[23]Who remembered us in our lowly state, for His mercy endures forever; [24]and rescued us from our enemies, for His mercy endures forever; [25]who gives food to all flesh, for His mercy endures forever. [26]Oh, give thanks to the God of heaven! For His mercy endures forever.*

Amen

Father, Your love is eternal. It stretches from west to east, from earth to heaven, just as Your Word declares. Jesus Christ said, "The Father loves you, and I love you." Lord, we thank You for Your everlasting love. We are grateful, Father, that even as the Creator of the heavens, the earth, and all that is in them, Your love remains constant and unchanging. Lord, You have placed Your Holy Spirit in the hearts of all who believe in You, and we thank

You for this extraordinary gift—this guarantee of our salvation: the Holy Spirit.

Holy Spirit, we thank You for Your love, goodness, and guidance—for leading us each day and cleansing our hands and feet, which are daily stained by this world. Lord, we are grateful and place ourselves at Your feet, asking that You work in each of us today. Draw us closer to You, Jesus Christ, and shape us more into Your image, Jesus Christ, and help us, Lord, to always give thanks in all things and to praise You, to lift Your name high, and to glorify only You in every storm and hardship.

Lord, help Iran and the Iranian people so that they too may lift up Your holy name and see Your love in all things. In times of hardship, in turmoil, even in the killings and darkness that are unfolding, we thank You, Lord, and declare that You are fully aware of everything. You are the one who will save us, the one who will lift us from our humiliation. You, Lord, are the one who will deliver us from the hands of oppressors and tyrants.

Lord, You are the one who will deliver and save Iran and its people. We have faith in You, and our joy comes from this. We praise You in every moment, for everything is in Your hands; You are the Creator of all things, and You are all-powerful. Your love is everlasting, and You will never take it away from us.

Father, pour out Your love and grace upon each one of us today. We place this day in Your blessed hands. Lord, heal the sick among us, heal our hearts, and heal the broken hearts of our people in Iran. Father, deliver them from their humiliation and from the hands of the oppressors and unjust, O Lord.

Lord, bind up the broken hearts, Father, and just as You have started Your work, bring it to completion.

Free Iran, the Iranian people, and each one of us from the evil one, Father. Jesus Christ, complete the work You have begun in

Iran and in each of us, so that we all may come to understand the height, width, and depth of Your love and mercy, Father. We place this day in Your blessed hands, for Your love is everlasting,

Amen

# Fifty-Fifth Day
## Father, we will be glad and rejoice in You

Our devotional today is from Psalm 9. Once again, we enter the presence of our Lord, lifting our voices in gratitude and thanksgiving:

*¹I will praise You, O Lord, with my whole heart; I will tell of all Your marvelous works. ²I will be glad and rejoice in You; I will sing praise to Your name, O Most High. ³When my enemies turn back; they shall fall and perish at Your presence. ⁴For You have maintained my right and my cause; You sat on the throne judging in righteousness. ⁵You have rebuked the nations, You have destroyed the wicked; You have blotted out their name forever and ever. ⁶O enemy, destructions are finished forever! And you have destroyed cities; even their memory has perished. ⁷But the Lord shall endure forever; He has prepared His throne for judgment. ⁸He shall judge the world in righteousness, and He shall administer judgment for the peoples in uprightness. ⁹The Lord also will be a refuge for the oppressed, a refuge in times of trouble. ¹⁰And those who know Your name will put their trust in You; for You, Lord, have not forsaken those who seek You. ¹¹Sing praises to the Lord, who dwells in Zion! Declare His deeds among the people. ¹²When He avenges blood, He remembers them; He does not forget the cry of the humble.*

Amen, Amen

Yes, Father. We see Your work every day. Open our eyes, Lord, so that in every situation and circumstance, we may recognize Your mighty, powerful, and loving hand at work. Let us see and understand that You are a just God, slow to anger and full of compassion. You, Father, show mercy to all, but Lord, Your beloved and cherished ones are the righteous—those who know

You and call upon Your name. Even those who don't know You are sincerely seeking You with all their hearts.

Father, we thank You and once again affirm that the entire world bears witness to Your name, and You judge with fairness. You are the One who destroys the wicked and all evil. A time will come when You erase even their names, while You will lift up the righteous and the saints, bringing freedom. You are the One who hears the cries of the oppressed. You are the One who, in times of distress, becomes a stronghold for all of us—a high fortress, so firm that no one can even touch it. Blessed are those who are under Your wings and within Your fortress, for their safety is eternal.

And we thank You, Lord Jesus Christ, for shedding Your blood on the cross for us. You opened our eyes to recognize that we are sinners, and You helped us come to You, ask for forgiveness, and plead for You to remove our sins and curses. You are so faithful, good, kind, full of grace and mercy, that You took all of them away, cleansed us, and brought us into Your kingdom and family. You brought us into Your strong and high fortress. Father, all those who are truly seeking You, and who are wholeheartedly desiring You but still do not know who You are—those who are searching for the true God but do not yet know You by name—Father, Son, and Holy Spirit, they have not seen You yet. Lord Jesus Christ, reveal Yourself to them.

As You are doing, we hear numerous testimonies from Muslims who share how You revealed Yourself to them in dreams and visions, drawing them toward You because they were seeking the true God in their hearts. You, Lord, are the one who sees the heart and never lets anyone lose hope. Our hope is in You, for You, Christ, are the Lord of love and compassion.

Lord, today, pour Your love and compassion upon each of us. Let us remember to praise and give thanks to You in every circumstance, for You are trustworthy, good, kind, and full of grace, and all things in You will be done with goodness.

We entrust today, our country Iran, the Iranian people, and the oppressed into Your blessed hands, asking, Lord, to bring freedom, peace, and comfort upon Iran, its people, and each of us.

In the name of Jesus Christ,

Amen

# Fifty-Sixth Day
## Lord grant us Your grace

In today's devotional, we meditate on Psalm 9:

*[13]Have mercy on me, O Lord! Consider my trouble from those who hate me, You who lift me up from the gates of death, [14]that I may tell of all Your praise in the gates of the daughter of Zion. I will rejoice in Your salvation. [15]The nations have sunk down in the pit which they made; in the net which they hid, their own foot is caught. [16]The Lord is known by the judgment He executes; the wicked is snared in the work of his own hands. Meditation. Selah. [17]The wicked shall be turned into hell, and all the nations that forget God. [18]For the needy shall not always be forgotten; the expectation of the poor shall not perish forever. [19]Arise, O Lord, do not let man prevail; let the nations be judged in Your sight. [20]Put them in fear, O Lord, that the nations may know themselves to be but men. Selah.*

Amen

Yes, Father. Father, pour out Your grace upon us, Lord, upon us who, through Jesus Christ and His blood, are Your children; He who brought us into Your family; and also upon Iran and the Iranian people. Lord, we stand as intercessors, partnering with Your Holy Spirit as mediators between darkness and light, O Lord. So, Father, look upon us. Look upon Iran, the Iranian people, and the situation of each of us, O Lord.

We know, O Lord, that You are the one who lifts us up, especially those of us who have accepted You, Jesus Christ, as Lord. You have redeemed us with Your blood from the gates of death and darkness. Lord, Jesus Christ, pour out Your grace upon Iran and the Iranian people as well and deliver them from the gates of death, so that they too may rise, lift Your name, give thanks to

You, and speak of Your mighty works, just as we, Your children, always proclaim and honor Your great works.

O Lord, we know that those who set traps and do evil will fall into their own snares and pits, because You are a kind and just God who judges righteously. Therefore, Lord, remove the hand of the wicked from each of us, from Iran, and from the Iranian people, O Father. Father, Your Word says that the needy will never be forgotten and are always in Your sight.

Father, rise up, O Lord, rise up and bring justice to the oppressed people, to the hearts of each of us, to our broken hearts, and to all the people of Iran, O Lord. Heal, Father, heal. Raise up, O God, a leader who can guide Iran toward freedom from the wicked and lead it to salvation.

O Lord, You have the power to complete the work You have begun in each of us. May we remember Your wonderful deeds at every moment, praise You, and give You thanks, for You are worthy of praise and deserving of worship.

We come before You with gratitude and praise. You know all our needs, O Lord; as Your word says, before we even speak, You have already heard our needs and You are aware of them. Nothing is hidden from You, O Father. Today, complete Your work in each of us. Bring freedom, peace, love, health, and comfort to the lives of each of us, to Iran, and to the Iranian people.

In the name of Jesus Christ,

Amen

# Fifty-Seventh Day
## The Lord Is the strength of our hearts

Our devotional today is from Psalm 10:

*¹Why do You stand afar off, O Lord? Why do You hide in times of trouble? ²The wicked in his pride persecutes the poor; let them be caught in the plots which they have devised. ³For the wicked boasts of his heart's desire; He blesses the greedy and renounces the Lord. ⁴The wicked in his proud countenance does not seek God; God is in none of his thoughts. ⁵His ways are always prospering; Your judgments are far above, out of his sight; as for all his enemies, he sneers at them. ⁶He has said in his heart, "I shall not be moved; I shall never be in adversity." ⁷His mouth is full of cursing and deceit and oppression; under his tongue is trouble and iniquity. ⁸He sits in the lurking places of the villages; in the secret places he murders the innocent; His eyes are secretly fixed on the helpless. ⁹He lies in wait secretly, as a lion in his den; He lies in wait to catch the poor; He catches the poor when he draws him into his net. ¹⁰So he crouches, he lies low, that the helpless may fall by his strength. ¹¹He has said in his heart, "God has forgotten; He hides His face; He will never see." ¹²Arise, O Lord! O God, lift up Your hand! Do not forget the humble. ¹³Why do the wicked renounce God? He has said in his heart, "You will not require an account."¹⁴but You have seen, for You observe trouble and grief, to repay it by Your hand. The helpless commits himself to You; You are the helper of the fatherless. ¹⁵Break the arm of the wicked and the evil man; seek out his wickedness until You find none. ¹⁶The Lord is King forever and ever; the nations have perished out of His land. ¹⁷Lord, You have heard the desire of the humble; You will prepare their heart; You will cause Your ear to hear, ¹⁸to do justice to the fatherless and the oppressed, that the man of the earth may oppress no more.*

Amen

Yes, Father, You are the Lord who sees everything. Today, we praise You and exalt Your name, for nothing is hidden from Your eyes or ears. You see everything and hear everything, O Lord. You are aware of the suffering of the oppressed, the orphans, the widows, and the broken-hearted. You, Father, and only You, are the healer of the souls of all the afflicted and suffering.

You, Jesus Christ, are the One who told us that You would never leave us alone in the storms and that You are always with us. Father, we know that You are alive; we know that You have not hidden your eyes, and we know that You have not stood by as a spectator. Rather, O Lord, You are at work. Dear Christ, through Your death on the cross and Your resurrection, You triumphed over death and Satan, and You continue to be victorious. And we, who are in You, are victorious as well.

Therefore, we are not afraid, O Lord, and we are not worried. We know our future is in Your hands, O Jesus Christ. Our future is in Your hands, O Father, and You desire the best for us, You desire the best for the land of Iran. O Lord, we know that You have heard and will hear the cries of each of our hearts, the cries of the heart of Iran and its people, and we know that You have begun a great work in Iran and will bring it to completion.

This is our hope and joy as we praise You, saying, 'Father, carry out Your work. Remove the wicked from Iran and free Iran, its people, and each of us.' Today, O Lord, search our hearts and remove anything that does not belong to You. Set fire to and destroy the strongholds of the wicked within us. Pour Your Holy Spirit more and more into us and fill us, Iran, and its people. As You have prophesied, establish Your throne over Iran and reign. O Lord, make Iran the first Christian nation in the Middle East.

We pray in the name of Jesus Christ, our Lord, and entrust this week into Your blessed hands. Strengthen us in our faith and deepen our zeal for You, making us strong and stronger.

Amen

# Fifty-Eight Day
## The Lord's eyes are watching

Our devotional today is based on Psalm 11:

*¹In the Lord I put my trust; how can you say to my soul, "flee as a bird to your mountain"? ²For look! The wicked bend their bow, they make ready their arrow on the string, that they may shoot secretly at the upright in heart. ³If the foundations are destroyed, what can the righteous do? ⁴The Lord is in His holy temple, the Lord's throne is in heaven; His eyes behold, His eyelids test the sons of men. ⁵The Lord tests the righteous, but the wicked and the one who loves violence His soul hates. ⁶Upon the wicked He will rain coals, fire and brimstone and a burning wind shall be the portion of their cup. ⁷For the Lord is righteous, He loves righteousness; His countenance beholds the upright.*

Amen

Yes, Father. We come before the Lord today and offer today into the presence of the Lord, seeking His blessing and love. Father, we are grateful that Your eyes are open and that You see everything, O Lord. Father, in times when we are down, in places where we witness wickedness and violence, where we long to escape to a place free from evil and bloodshed, You tell us to find peace in You. You say, *"Come to Me, all you who are burdened, and lay your burdens down, and I will give you rest. Take My yoke upon you, for My yoke is easy"*.

O Jesus Christ, today we come before You, bringing our heavy burdens and laying them at Your feet. We say, O Jesus Christ, take all of this away. You paid the price for all our sins and curses on the cross. Through Your blood and resurrection, You freed us and brought us into the kingdom of God. May You free all the people of Iran, both spiritually and physically.

Lord, Your throne stands firm from eternity to eternity. Your kingdom remains unshaken. You are steadfast, unchanging, and unwavering. You speak to us, declaring, *"Jesus Christ is the same yesterday, today, and forever"*. You have promised to always be with us and never forsake us. So, Lord, we trust that You are with us today. We know it, Lord.

Father, we bring our sick before You. Place Your healing hand upon them, restore them, and lift them up, Lord. We present to You Iran, its people, the grieving, the oppressed, and those who have suffered injustice. None are hidden from Your sight, and You despise violence and wrongdoing.

So, Lord, bring freedom, love, purity, and peace—everything You have promised—to each of us, to Iran, and to every Iranian, for You are always faithful to Your promises.

Gracious and compassionate Father, we entrust this day to You. Accomplish Your work, pour out Your healing, love, and grace upon us, and use each of us today for the fulfillment of Your Kingdom. Rescue Iran and its people, Lord.

In the name of Jesus Christ,

Amen

# Fifty-Ninth Day
## The words of the Lord are pure words

Our devotional today is from Psalm 12:

*¹Help, Lord, for the godly man ceases! For the faithful disappear from among the sons of men. ²They speak idly everyone with his neighbor; with flattering lips and a double heart they speak. ³May the Lord cut off all flattering lips, and the tongue that speaks proud things, ⁴who have said, "with our tongue we will prevail; our lips are our own; who is lord over us?" ⁵"For the oppression of the poor, for the sighing of the needy, now I will arise," says the Lord; "I will set him in the safety for which he yearns." ⁶The words of the Lord are pure words, like silver tried in a furnace of earth, purified seven times. ⁷You shall keep them, O Lord, You shall preserve them from this generation forever. ⁸The wicked prowl on every side, when vileness is exalted among the sons of men.*

Amen. Amen

Father, we thank You and are grateful for a new day, a good day, where we can come before You and share the deepest desires of our hearts. Today, Lord, we come to You and declare that You are a God full of love, grace, and hope. Father, when the wicked, the deceitful, and the flatterers surround us, we turn to You and pour out our hearts before You.

Your Word says that You are a God who sees everything—you see the oppression of the afflicted, You see the needs of the vulnerable, and You hear their cries. So, Father, we ask You to do Your work in each of us today.

You have promised that if we seek first the kingdom of God, all these things—all our needs and everything we lack—will be provided for us. Therefore, we seek You first, we desire You, and we long for Your will to be done in every area of our lives, in our hearts, in our thoughts, and in our decisions today. Lord, may Your will be accomplished in all of these things today.

Dear Holy Spirit, guide each of us today so that in every word we speak, every action we take, and every decision we make, we may first seek to honor Your kingdom and exalt Your name, Lord. May we never do anything that would bring shame or dishonor to You, because You, Lord, are compassionate, merciful, just, and filled with goodness.

So, Lord, respond to our hearts— the hearts of the people of Iran, the oppressed, the mourning mothers, the grieving fathers, the lost brothers and sisters, and the anguished hearts of those in need. As Your word declares today, You will not only intervene but will also establish them in the security for which they long.

Therefore, our hope is in You, knowing that You detest oppression, injustice, flattery, and deceit, and none of these can stand in Your presence. Lord, deliver each of us from the grip of flattery, falsehood, and oppression, and rescue Iran and its people from the hands of the oppressors, the wicked, and the deceitful.

In the name of Jesus Christ,

Amen

# Sixtieth Day
## In Your presence Father, is fullness of joy

Our devotional today is from Psalm 16: 5-11:

*⁵O Lord, You are the portion of my inheritance and my cup; You maintain my lot. ⁶The lines have fallen to me in pleasant places; yes, I have a good inheritance. ⁷I will bless the Lord who has given me counsel; my heart also instructs me in the night seasons. ⁸I have set the Lord always before me; because He is at my right hand I shall not be moved. ⁹Therefore my heart is glad, and my glory rejoices; my flesh also will rest in hope. ¹⁰For You will not leave my soul in Sheol, nor will You allow Your Holy One to see corruption. ¹¹You will show me the path of life; in Your presence is fullness of joy; at Your right hand are pleasures forevermore.*

Amen. Amen

Yes, Lord. Yes, Father. You are the portion and cup of each one of us. You are a righteous God who upholds the inheritance of us, the inheritance of the believers, the oppressed, and the orphaned. O Father, You are the One who lifts us up in the end, grants us a great inheritance, and fills our hearts with joy and gladness.

Today, Lord, we choose joy and gladness in You. We choose to worship and praise You, Father, Jesus Christ. We come before You in worship and praise, declaring that You alone are holy and deserving of all praise and worship. We thank You, Lord, for Your goodness. We give thanks to You, Father, for Your unfailing love. We are grateful to You, Jesus Christ, for Your grace and for shedding Your blood on the cross for all humanity. We thank You for saving us and for Your resurrection, through which You triumphed over evil, darkness, and death. And we are grateful that in You, we have victory.

Yes, Lord, Your Word prophesies that You will not allow the body of Jesus Christ to undergo decay but will raise Him up—and You will also lift us up with Him, not letting our bodies be cast into Hell. You will not let the people of Iran or the land of Iran be cast into the abyss. Lord, You are always faithful to Your promises to each of us who acknowledge You, Jesus Christ, and recognize You as our Savior and Lord.

You have saved us. Lord, You declare that today we are seated with You in the heavens at Your right hand. And if we are at Your right hand and all things are in Your control, what do we have to fear? We have no fear, and our joy and gladness will endure forever because You are always with us and will never forsake us.

Lord, help us never to forget this truth and to always remember, even in times of hardship and turmoil, that You are with us and that all things will come together for good. We know, Lord, that You hear each of us—the people of Iran and the cry of the nation—and that everything is in Your hands, O Father.

Jesus Christ, You have established and will continue to establish Your throne over Iran, securing it firmly, and according to Your promise, You will set Iran and its people free. So, Lord, bring this to fulfillment without delay and deliver us and the people of Iran from the grip of the wicked. May we continually lift Your name in praise, keep our hearts and minds fixed on You throughout this day. May we seek Your will in all things, and dedicate ourselves to the work of Your kingdom.

In the name of Jesus Christ,

Amen

www.ingramcontent.com/pod-product-compliance
Lightning Source LLC
Chambersburg PA
CBHW051319120626
46547CB00015B/2302

* 9 7 8 1 9 7 0 8 6 4 3 6 6 *